beginning your journey toward lasting change

WORKBOOK

STEPS

TYNDALE
REFRESH™
Think Well. Live Well. Be Well.

JOHN ORTBERG
ALYSSA CHANDLER

Visit Tyndale online at tyndale.com.

Visit Tyndale Christian Resources online at tyndalechristianresources.com.

Please visit the author online at becomenew.com.

Tyndale Refresh is a nonfiction imprint of Tyndale House Publishers, Carol Stream, Illinois.

Steps Workbook: Beginning Your Journey Toward Lasting Change

Cover illustration and design by Dean H. Renninger

Interior design by Brandi Davis

Edited by Jonathan Schindler

For information about special discounts for bulk purchases, please contact Tyndale House Publishers at csresponse@tyndale.com, or call 1-855-277-9400.

ISBN 979-8-4005-2474-5

Printed in the United States of America

32 31 30 29 28 27 26
7 6 5 4 3 2 1

Contents

Contents

Introduction

Thank you for choosing to take the next step in your twelve-step journey with this workbook. We're so glad you're here.

This workbook is meant to accompany *Steps: A Guide to Transforming Your Life When Willpower Isn't Enough* by John Ortberg. *Steps* and this workbook are designed to help you practice the Twelve Steps as a program for life and spiritual formation. The Twelve Steps of Alcoholics Anonymous are not only for alcoholics or addicts, as many envision them. The Twelve Steps are a framework for spiritual formation. The truth is, if you are a human being with a pulse, you are a hopeless addict. "We are all overly attached to something—starting with our egos—that we are powerless to control" (*Steps*, 8).

The workbook you're holding has twelve sections, mirroring the Twelve Steps covered in the *Steps* book. As you read *Steps*, you can stop after each step (and its subchapters) to go deeper into practical application, using this workbook as a guide. There are QR codes at the beginning of each section of this workbook. If you scan the codes, you will be able to access the video curriculum John teaches on each step to go deeper into the book's ideas.

Every section of this workbook includes the same elements: some short opening thoughts and a prayer, a video that walks you through the step, and questions for either group discussion or self-reflection. Then you'll find activities to help you put the step into practice. These activities are where the rubber meets the road, but you don't have to complete them all—feel free to respond to only the ones that feel applicable to you. Finally, we provide relevant Scripture, closing thoughts, and a journal space for reflection.

If you're engaging with this study in a small group, we recommend having one person play the video for all participants and then using the teachings as a launching point for discussion. (For more, see "Leader Tips" on page 3.)

John writes in *Steps* that it "is written for anyone hungry for more, whether you have an identified addiction or not. It is not a 'recovery' book. It's written to help *anyone* enter into an actionable, non-legalistic, spiritual way of life that—oh, by the way—has had the empirically verified side effect of freeing millions of people from addictions when random 'spirituality' could not" (page 7).

Sound like it could help? We think so too. Let's get to work.

Leader Tips

The following tips will help you as you lead your group through the *Steps Workbook.*

BEFORE THE SESSION

- Watch the video and look over the discussion questions and key activities in the workbook in advance of the meeting.
- Pray by name for each person who will be attending. Ask that God would help them carry out the steps with honesty and vulnerability.
- Consider arranging food for the session. Snacks can loosen the atmosphere and make people more comfortable with sharing. Bonus points if you serve stale coffee and donuts, like an AA meeting (kidding).
- Encourage participants to read the appropriate chapters in *Steps* before you meet.

AT THE SESSION

- Welcome each person to the group when they arrive and carry that spirit of warmth throughout the session.
- Play the video teaching for the group and encourage them to take notes in their workbooks. (You can scan the QR code in each chapter

to access the video for that step, or you can find all the videos at becomenew.com/steps.)

- Encourage each person to speak during the discussion. Don't leave anyone out.
- Don't be afraid to adapt the material provided in this study—cutting questions or lingering on a topic—to provide the best experience for your group.
- Be mindful of participants' time and do your best to keep the study within the parameters you've set for the group. That being said, if the Holy Spirit is moving, do what you can to allow extra time and space to minister.
- Remind participants of the activities that accompany each session, which can be accomplished throughout the week. Highlight one or more of these activities and request reports at your next session.
- Consider taking prayer requests at the close of your session or breaking into smaller groups for prayer.

STEP 1

The Problem: I Can't

We admitted we were powerless over our deepest problems—
that our lives had become unmanageable.

STEPS, PAGES 1–32

OPENING REFLECTION

Steps and this workbook are designed to help you practice the Twelve Steps as a program for life and spiritual formation. The Twelve Steps of Alcoholics Anonymous are not only for addicts in the traditional sense. They are a framework for spiritual formation. The truth is, if you are a human being with a pulse, you are a hopeless addict. As John writes, "We are all overly attached to something—starting with our egos—that we are powerless to control" (*Steps*, 8).

Step 1 says this plainly, right off the bat: We are powerless. We can't control our life. They have become unmanageable for us on our own.

We can't control our life, but God can. (We'll get into that in Step 2.)

So before we begin, let's pause to pray together:

God, as I enter this space, help me to be honest with myself, with others, and with you. Meet me in my weakness. Show me that it is okay to be powerless because I am not God. And thank God for that. Amen.

VIDEO NOTES

As you watch the video, use the space below to take notes. We've included some key points to get you started.

SCAN HERE TO WATCH THE VIDEO FOR STEP 1.

Step 1 is about admitting powerlessness at the core, gut level of who we are.

In AA, this deep experience is sometimes called "the gift of desperation" because it becomes the very thing that leads us to God.

A wimpy Step 1 leads to wimpy Steps 2 through 12. Experiencing powerlessness is what opens us to transformation.

"The recognition and public acknowledgment of personal inadequacy is a spiritual achievement that must be ritualized and celebrated." (Paraphrased from Kent Dunnington, *Addiction and Virtue* [IVP Academic, 2025], 186.)

Scripture is full of people experiencing this step:

- Acts 2 (the people of Jerusalem)
- Luke 5 (Simon Peter)
- Isaiah 6 (Isaiah)
- Romans 7 (Paul)

A key to spiritual growth that's present in addiction is unforced, desperate awareness of need.

Step 1 is the foundation of spiritual life for everybody.

We don't end up in hopelessness, but we start there.

DISCUSSION QUESTIONS

Use these questions to discuss in a small group or reflect individually in your workbook.

1. In terms of powerlessness, how much or how little do you believe your life is unmanageable on your own right now? Why did you answer this way?

2. The Big Book of Alcoholics Anonymous says that acceptance is the answer to all our problems. Does that resonate with you today? Why or why not?

3. What is one significant reality in your life that you often resist accepting? Why?

4. John writes, "AA got the Twelve Steps from the church. And now the church needs them back" (*Steps*, 7). Think of a time when you hid parts of yourself from others in the church out of fear or shame. Why did you do this?

5. Step 1 helps us break through denial and accept reality. It helps us become willing to change. So . . . on a scale of 1–10, how willing to change do you feel today? Explain the number you chose.

KEY ACTIVITIES

Naming Powerlessness

The first step is the only one we're told we must do perfectly: *Admit we are powerless*. In *Steps*, John begins by acknowledging that all sorts of things—from family, job, and reputation to friends, temper, and money; from the silly or mundane to the serious and deeply troubling—are beyond our control (see page 1). This honesty is painful, but it's the door into freedom for all of us.

Take a moment to write down three "I can't . . ." statements for yourself. Don't fix or explain them—just consider and then write.

1. I can't ________________________________.
2. I can't ________________________________.
3. I can't ________________________________.

Admitting It

Writer Stephen Haynes describes Step 0 like this: "We admitted that, despite all appearances, we were not fine" (*Steps*, 15). For many of us—especially those of us in religious settings—this may be the hardest confession. We want to appear spiritually mature. We want to maintain an image of holiness and put-together-ness.

But God deals in honesty, not appearances. Pretending is a lie, and it only keeps us trapped. So Step 1 is not just an intellectual agreement; it's a gut-level acknowledgment of inadequacy. We have to do this with our whole heart.

Try this as a prayer: *God, I admit that, despite all appearances, I am not fine.*

How does saying those words make you feel? Write down or share your experience with others.

Addressing Shame

Stigma marked culture in Jesus' time on earth, and it's still part of society today (see *Steps*, 13). But Jesus turns stigma into welcome. The Fellowship of the Withered Hand is not a community of people who are perfectly polished and put-together. It's a fellowship of the broken.

Sociologist Erving Goffman wrote that the word *stigma* used to refer to the brand marking a disgraced individual as either a criminal or a slave (see *Steps*, 13). Jesus himself bore a stigma in the wounds of the cross. Those same scars became his glory.

What scar in your life do you see as shame?

How might it become a place of strength in God's hands?

Your Withered Hand

John invites you to identify your own place of powerlessness (see *Steps*, 16). This is the beginning of the Fellowship of the Withered Hand: a community where brokenness is not hidden but revealed and celebrated. It's the inadequacy that unites us. "What God asks us to do—what we know we *should* do—is precisely what we are unable to do" (*Steps*, 12).

What part of yourself do you most want to hide?

How might God be inviting you to bring it into the open?

Pray simply, *God, here is my withered hand. I cannot stretch it out without you.*

Manageability

Chapter 1B challenges us to consider what "unmanageable" really means. It's not just about crisis; it's about realizing self-will is not enough. John writes, "Our lives are unmanageable. We have all been idiots and will be idiots again. It *is* 'that bad'" (*Steps*, 20).

Rate each area of your life from 1 to 5 (1 = not manageable at all; 5 = completely manageable).

- Thought life: __/5
- Emotions: __/5
- Words/mouth: __/5
- Habits/impulses: __/5
- Time/money: __/5

Which number surprised you most?

Which one do you sense God wants to bring clarity to first?

Acceptance

On pages 27–28, *Steps* introduces a tool called the Scale of Acceptance for recognizing your feelings about the circumstances in your life. You can use this scale to locate your feelings about anything you are powerless over.

It goes like this:

SCALE OF ACCEPTANCE

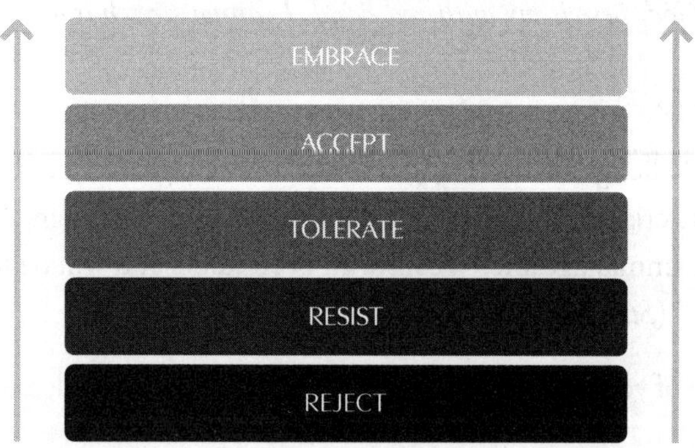

Consider the items below:

- My inadequacy (name it): ________________________
- Where I am on the scale: ________________
- One step I can take to move up: ________________

Pray: *God, help me move one step closer to embracing the place where I need you most.*

SCRIPTURE FOR REFLECTION

Use this section to reflect on some verses that shed light on this step. You might ask God to reveal what he wants you to take away from them.

> On another Sabbath day, a man with a deformed right hand was in the synagogue while Jesus was teaching. The teachers of religious law and the Pharisees watched Jesus closely. If he healed the man's hand, they planned to accuse him of working on the Sabbath.
>
> But Jesus knew their thoughts. He said to the man with the deformed hand, "Come and stand in front of everyone." So the man came forward. Then Jesus said to his critics, "I have a question for you. Does the law permit good deeds on the Sabbath, or is it a day for doing evil? Is this a day to save life or to destroy it?"
>
> He looked around at them one by one and then said to the man, "Hold out your hand." So the man held out his hand, and it was restored! At this, the enemies of Jesus were wild with rage and began to discuss what to do with him.
>
> **LUKE 6:6-11**

What details stand out in this story?

Why do you think Jesus asked the man to reveal his weakness publicly?

> I take pleasure in my weaknesses, and in the insults, hardships, persecutions, and troubles that I suffer for Christ. For when I am weak, then I am strong.
>
> **2 CORINTHIANS 12:10**

What words or phrases stand out?

Can you think of a time your weakness felt like strength? What happened?

CLOSING THOUGHTS

As you embark on this journey through the Twelve Steps, remember that we begin recovery not in strength but in powerlessness. When we feel vulnerable or uneasy or even uncomfortably seen, we are getting somewhere! Often naming our "withered hand" is the first act of honesty that unlocks the rest of the process.

The most frequently asked question is, "How long will it take me to tackle the steps?"

The answer will frustrate you. Ready?

This will take your whole life. (How's that for a commitment?) It's an ongoing, continuous process that will reveal where your heart truly lies and will open up a pathway to fellowship with God like you've never experienced.

The Fellowship of the Withered Hand is a community where weakness is strength. Inadequacy is welcome. No one has it all figured out.

And you are invited.

So keep reading. As they say in AA, "Keep coming back. It works if you work it."

JOURNAL SPACE

After completing this section, take five to ten minutes of silence. Then think through these questions in the journaling space that follows:

- What do I sense God saying to me through this material?
- What part(s) of me am I ready to bring into the open?
- What next step will I take?

STEP 2

The Solution: He Can

We came to believe that a Power greater than ourselves could restore us to sanity.

STEPS, PAGES 33–56

OPENING REFLECTION

Step 1 is all about admitting powerlessness. It can be summarized by the words "I can't." John writes, "With that admission came helplessness and despair. We have no hope in ourselves" (*Steps*, 35).

This brings us to Step 2. This step *begins* with hope. It can be summarized in two simple words: "He can."

On our own, we are deeply inadequate. However, our inadequacy doesn't need to be the end of our story (see *Steps*, 39). Because of God's power, because of his love and care and grace, difficult circumstances aren't cause for despair. Instead, they can become a crucible where we experience God's manifest presence.

In Step 2, we get to think about possibility. We move from despair to belief. Instead of clinging to the words "I can't," we realize and triumph in the fact that "God can."

So that's what this step will entail: putting our faith in God rather than ourselves. Before we move farther, let's pause and pray:

> *God, we can't, but you can. Help us to have eyes to see where we've stopped believing you are in control. You are our ultimate helper. Help us remember that through any situation we face, you're with us. Restore to us the sanity of trust in you. Amen.*

VIDEO NOTES

As you watch the video, use the space below to take notes. We've included some key points to get you started.

SCAN HERE TO WATCH THE VIDEO FOR STEP 2.

Step 2 is where hope enters the picture: "I can't . . . but God can."

Each step is written in the past tense because they worked before they got codified.

Faith without works is dead. Faith is coming to believe that Jesus' way is the only sane and rational way to live. And there is power from him to live this kind of life.

Faith is a process: We came . . . We came to . . . We came to believe.

Sanity means living in reality. There is one God, and it is not you.

Get honest with yourself, because we're meeting in the basement together.

DISCUSSION QUESTIONS

Use these questions to discuss in a small group or reflect individually in your workbook.

1. Who is a person in your life that deepens your belief in God and confirms that he is worth giving your life to? What about them makes you feel this way? If you don't have someone in your life like that, what's one way you could move toward identifying someone who could model faith for you?

2. What scenario in your life most often causes you to say, "But I . . ." instead of "But God . . ."?

3. Are there any areas of your life in which you've given up hope? Why? What could it look like to "come to believe" again?

4. John writes about a "good-enough" faith (see *Steps*, 43–46). What could that look like in your life?

5. Have you ever heard the phrase "restore us to sanity"? What does it mean to you? How can you become a lover of reality today?

KEY ACTIVITIES

But God . . .

In *Steps*, John writes about how both the Bible and human life center around two words: "But God" (see *Steps*, 37–40).

However, we can get caught up in "But I . . ." statements, forgetting who is really in control. Let's take a few minutes now to write down the "But I . . ." statements we typically fall prey to, and then we'll rewrite them into the "But God . . ." statements they were always meant to be.

Here are a few examples to get you started.

- But I am too afraid. → But God can calm my fears.
- But I don't know how to fix this. → But God is still on the throne.

Now try it on your own:

- But I ______________________. → But God ______________________.
- But I ______________________. → But God ______________________.
- But I ______________________. → But God ______________________.

Sanity by Definition

John writes, "*Sanity* is not about IQ or even the absence of emotional distress. It is soundness of mind, healthy perspective, good judgment, freedom from impulsivity, the ability to place what is good and right over what we happen to desire" (*Steps*, 46).

Isn't it amazing how we can sometimes convince ourselves of things that are false, denying reality and protecting ourselves from the truth? Insulating our ego and mind in this way can prevent us from healing.

So right now, answer the following prompts, and then write out a definition for sanity in your own words.

Where do you feel like your life, emotionally or spiritually, might be off-balance?

How might it change your perspective to bring God into that area?

Here's what sanity means to me:

Assess Your Faith

John writes about a faith that develops in stages. First we *came*, then we *came to*, and finally we *came to believe* (see *Steps*, 46). There is great intention and meaning in this progression.

"We came" means simply showing up, maybe having a curious spirit and a willingness to learn.

"We came to" is awakening. This is the realization that we need help. We can't do this alone.

And finally, "we came to believe." This is the beginning of our trust in God's faithfulness. He is good. We need him in this process.

So with those stages in mind, take a moment to honestly assess. Of the options below, where do you fall on the scale?

__ I'm just showing up. I'm simply in the "we came" stage of the progression.

__ I'm becoming aware that I need help in my life. I'm awake—"we came to."

__ I'm starting to believe. God is in control of my life. "We came to believe."

Take a moment to write down any thoughts about your response above.

Core Doubts

On pages 46–48 in *Steps*, John identifies several common doubts that take hold within us. Look at the list below, then circle the doubt that resonates most with you. Or maybe for you it's doubtfulness about something else entirely. If that's the case, fill in the blank with your area of doubt.

- Doubting that God has power
- Doubting that God is good
- Doubting that God exists
- Doubting that God intervenes
- Doubting that people change
- Doubting religion
- Doubting that ______________________________

What would happen if you brought that doubt honestly to God? Instead of fighting it or denying it inside, what if you held open your hands and surrendered it to him? Take a moment to journal about what could happen if you released that doubt into his care.

Be with Me

Chapter 2C ends with a simple invitation: "Today, each time you think of it, ask God to interact with you in guidance, inspiration, and love" (*Steps*, 55). We practice inviting God's presence into our life. Notice that we don't call it achieving, understanding, or mastering trust—this is a *practice*. The reason we use the word *practice* is because this is something we can get better at. Control may be alluring, but it's not serving us in the long run.

This week, pray the "be with me" prayer: *Lord, be with me in my thoughts. Be with me in my work. Be with me in my relationships. Amen.*

If you feel avoidant, don't fight it. Brother Lawrence, who wrote the classic book *The Practice of the Presence of God*, understood how you feel. He struggled deeply with feeling unloved and unseen by God (see *Steps*, 55). Maybe that's you too.

Right now, take some time to think about the last time you truly felt God's presence. Write down what it felt like, where you were, and how you got there. Consider even writing out the "be with me" prayer to invite him in right now.

SCRIPTURE FOR REFLECTION

Use this section to reflect on some verses that shed light on this step. You might ask God to reveal what he wants you to take away from them.

> My health may fail, and my spirit may grow weak,
> but God remains the strength of my heart;
> he is mine forever.
>
> **PSALM 73:26**

What does it mean to you for God to be your strength and yours forever?

> [The boy's father said,] "Have mercy on us and help us, if you can."
>
> "What do you mean, 'If I can'?" Jesus asked. "Anything is possible if a person believes."
>
> The father instantly cried out, "I do believe, but help me overcome my unbelief!"
>
> **MARK 9:22-24**

Is there any part of your life where you've been stuck believing a lie is true? Pray this verse as a prayer to God over that part of your story.

> The word of God will never fail.
>
> **LUKE 1:37**

This is a verse full of hope. Speak it over an area of your life where you might have lost confidence in God's provision and care for you.

CLOSING THOUGHTS

"I can't. He can."

Step 1 was about honesty, but Step 2 is about hope. The light is starting to break through. The truth is, you don't have to have it all figured out right now, or even feel any measure of certainty. All you have to do in this moment is be *willing* to believe that help can come from beyond you. From God.

This is where faith gets personal. It's the quiet, steady decision to let go of self-reliance and lean on God instead. If you've never been a believer before, you may find that faith doesn't happen overnight. Instead, it builds slowly over time. It happens through practicing "good-enough" faith.

So this week, that's what you can work on. You don't have to be flawless; you just have to try. Simply show up and seek God. Be open to him.

And if you're not sure you believe yet, that's okay. Keep showing up. Keep coming back. And there's good news: Step 3 gets fun. Spoiler: It can be summarized as "I think I'll let him."

This completes the full phrase of Steps 1 through 3: "I can't. He can. I think I'll let him."

There's our foundation. Keep coming back. It works if you work it.

JOURNAL SPACE

After completing this chapter, take five to ten minutes of silence. Then think through these questions in the journaling space that follows:

- What do I sense God saying to me through this material?
- Am I ready to "come to believe"?
- What is the next step I will take?

STEP 3

The Decision: I Think I'll Let Him

We made a decision to turn our will and our lives over to the care of God as we understood Him.

STEPS, PAGES 57–83

OPENING REFLECTION

As we discussed in the last sections, Step 1 is about honesty. It's where we admit that we can't do it. Our life is unmanageable, and we are powerless. Step 2 brings us to hope—we believe God *can* do it. That's good news. He's in charge of our life. There is a God, and we are not him.

Now, Step 3 brings us to surrender. In this step, we choose to place our trust in God. This is where faith becomes action. "Half measures availed us nothing" (more on this in *Steps*, 60–62). Step 3 serves as a reminder that, actually, we don't run the show. We aren't in charge of our life. We aren't God (and thank God for that). There's a quote from the miniseries *Band of Brothers* that captures this reality: "The only hope you have is to accept the fact that you're already dead" (*Steps*, 59).

In other words, as long as we try to retain control in our life and play the role that only God can, we are trapped. We are in despair. When we finally let go, though, and die to ourselves and our self-will, we come alive in an entirely new way. That's what this step is all about.

So now, before we continue, pause and pray:

God, thank you for this journey. I offer myself to you. Allow me to give you my desires, my will, and my tendency to act like God, and teach me to live with open hands. Help me to follow you and to turn my will over to your care. Amen.

VIDEO NOTES

As you watch the video, use the space below to take notes. We've included some key points to get you started.

SCAN HERE TO WATCH THE VIDEO FOR STEP 3.

In Step 3, we turn over two things to God: our will (our ability to choose) and our life (our circumstances).

The will is made to surrender to God.

Desire narrows our thinking.

Think about it: Which dimension of your life is the hardest for you to turn over to God?

Surrender is not passive.

What we turn over to God are the results of our actions, not the actions themselves.

The more we depend on God for our identity, the less we have to depend on our job status or marital status.

DISCUSSION QUESTIONS

Use these questions to discuss in a small group or reflect individually in your workbook.

1. Which parts of your life feel hardest for you to hand over to God's care?

2. Think of a time when you finally let go of control of an area of your life. What was that experience like for you? Did you find peace? Explain.

3. Step 3 reminds us that half measures avail us nothing. Do you have any personal half measures, where you give some parts of yourself over to God but not all? Name these half measures. What power do these half measures have over your life today?

4. Think about the addictions that have the tightest grip on your life. What are some indicators that you have slipped back into your will instead of actively surrendering when it comes to these behaviors or patterns?

5. What could it look like for you to choose to surrender your life and your will to God daily? How might you incorporate that practice into your everyday habits?

KEY ACTIVITIES

Half Measures

John discusses the concept of half measures on pages 60–62 of *Steps*. Half measures happen when we want God's will for our life but aren't quite sure we want to follow him fully. We aren't convinced that turning over our will, our choices, and our agenda will give us the results we want. We want to have our cake and eat it too: We long for safety but struggle with surrender. We crave control but want forgiveness and grace.

In this activity, we're seeking to name our half measures. Where are those places in our life where we have one foot in and one foot out? Take a few minutes to fill out the table below.

HALF MEASURE	FULL SURRENDER

Now, ask yourself which half measure feels the hardest to release fully. Why might that be?

Practicing Open Hands

In *Steps*, John quotes psychiatrist Gerald May on the difference between willingness and willfulness. May writes, "Willingness implies a surrendering of one's self-separateness, an entering-into, an immersion in the deepest processes of life itself. . . . In contrast, willfulness is the setting of oneself apart from the fundamental essence of life in an attempt to master, direct, control, or otherwise manipulate existence" (page 65).

John encourages us to physically experience both willfulness and willingness.

Right now, we'll go through the activity he outlines in the book. Make a fist with both hands. Squeeze as hard as you can. Feel the tension and notice how exhausting it is. *That's* willfulness.

Now . . . release your fists. Exhale. Let it all go. Feel the relief it brings.

That's willingness. Letting go of white knuckles and striving. Willingness is embracing. Surrendering. And there's great news: Willingness is always available with God.

Right now, consider an area of your life where you want to shift from willfulness to willingness. Write it down and then say a prayer that God would lovingly and gently help you open up your fists.

The Serenity Prayer

A cornerstone of AA is the Serenity Prayer. It's a wonderfully helpful and centering prayer to remind us that we are not ultimately in control. Read through the prayer below and meditate on it with God:

> *God, grant me the serenity*
> *to accept the things I cannot change,*
> *the courage to change the things I can,*
> *and the wisdom to know the difference.*
> *Living one day at a time,*
> *enjoying one moment at a time,*
> *accepting hardships as the pathway to peace,*
> *taking, as he did, this sinful world as it is,*
> *not as I would have it,*
> *trusting that he will make all things right*

if I surrender to his will—
that I may be reasonably happy in this life
and supremely happy with him forever.

What's one area of your life where you need God's wisdom to know the difference between what you can and can't change?

Surrender Versus Passivity

An important distinction: Surrender is not equivalent to apathy. It's not avoiding responsibility. Surrender is trusting God as you act. On page 72 in *Steps*, John gives us some examples of biblical figures who surrendered without being pushovers:

- Moses was not a doormat to Pharaoh.
- David was not a doormat to Goliath.
- Daniel was not a doormat to Nebuchadnezzar.
- Esther was not a doormat to Haman.
- Jesus was not a doormat to anyone.

Think of a time in your life when you lived in surrender. What was it like? What were the results?

Turn It Over. Take It Back.

Chapter 3C reminds us that surrender is a continuous, ongoing process (see *Steps*, 77–78). Often we give something over to God, then a few minutes pass, and it seems we've taken it back. So we start over. Wash, rinse, repeat.

Here is the cycle John outlines (*Steps*, 78):

1. I can't.
2. He can.
3. I think I'll let him.
4. Oops.
5. (Do it again.)

So what's the antidote to this madness? Take a deep breath and pray, *God, your will be done. Not mine. Amen.* Maybe even write it down here. Remember, this is a daily process.

Do the Opposite

As counterintuitive as it may seem, there is an antidote that can rewire our behavior patterns. It's a life strategy called "Do the Opposite" (see *Steps*, 78–81). It's taught by psychologist Marsha Linehan, and it's about acting against our old habits.

So, for example . . .

- If you're scared to talk to people, start a conversation with someone.
- If you're easily angered, forgive someone in the moment, when you are convinced they don't deserve it.
- If you're hiding something, readily confess it.

You get the picture. Actively choosing to oppose the behaviors we tend toward is living out this practice. And, funny enough, each of the Twelve Steps at their core involves doing the opposite of those emotion-driven, ego-charged choices that have gotten us into trouble. Remember, this is not about changing yourself but about practicing surrender when self-will shows up.

Think for a moment about a scenario in your life where you can practice doing the opposite. Write it down, and commit to breaking a pattern you know you want to change.

SCRIPTURE FOR REFLECTION

Use this section to reflect on some verses that shed light on this step. You might ask God to reveal what he wants you to take away from them.

> Mary responded, "I am the Lord's servant. May everything you have said about me come true." And then the angel left her.
>
> **LUKE 1:38**

What could Mary's kind of surrender look like in your life today?

> You must have the same attitude that Christ Jesus had.
>
> Though he was God,
>   he did not think of equality with God
>   as something to cling to.
> Instead, he gave up his divine privileges;
>   he took the humble position of a slave
>   and was born as a human being.

> When he appeared in human form,
> he humbled himself in obedience to God
> and died a criminal's death on a cross.
>
> **PHILIPPIANS 2:5-8**

How might you let go of control today and imitate Jesus' posture?

> Dear brothers and sisters, I plead with you to give your bodies to God because of all he has done for you. Let them be a living and holy sacrifice—the kind he will find acceptable. This is truly the way to worship him. Don't copy the behavior and customs of this world, but let God transform you into a new person by changing the way you think. Then you will learn to know God's will for you, which is good and pleasing and perfect.
>
> **ROMANS 12:1-2**

In which areas of your life is God inviting you to change your thinking about surrender?

CLOSING THOUGHTS

In this section, we learned that Step 3 is where the rubber meets the road. It's where belief turns into trust and trust becomes action.

Too often, we offer God slivers of our life. We give him a little here, a little there. But as we've learned, half measures avail us nothing. God loves us way too much for a partial surrender. That's why this step challenges us to turn our will and our life over to his care.

When we do finally give in and give him control, something in us shifts. We're not on the throne; Jesus is, and there's great peace in that truth.

This process doesn't happen overnight. It's a daily act of courage that slowly, steadily gets easier. And as we discussed, you'll surrender completely . . . and then find yourself taking it back.

That's okay. It's normal. Just trust the process and start over again.

Keep going. Keep coming back. Keep opening your hands.

"I can't. He can. I think I'll let him."

JOURNAL SPACE

After completing this chapter, take five to ten minutes of silence. Then think through these questions in the journaling space on the following page:

- What do I sense God saying to me through this material?
- Which part of this teaching was hardest for me to accept? Why might that be?
- Are there half measures in my life I wasn't consciously aware of before?
- What next step will I take now?

STEP 4

The Examination: A Fearless Inventory

We made a searching and fearless moral inventory of ourselves.

STEPS, PAGES 85–107

OPENING REFLECTION

So you've made it to Step 4. In this step, we patiently explore our motives, our habits, and our blind spots to see where we need to change. John explains in *Steps* that this can often be a part of the journey that causes many people to quit. It can be terrifying and painful to turn inward and take inventory of what's in our heart. As John puts it, "We all resist facing ugly truths about ourselves" (*Steps*, 87).

But as difficult as it is, it is a part of the journey toward healing. So we forge on together.

A few notes that will be helpful as you dive into this chapter: This step is not meant for self-condemnation. Don't shame yourself or wallow in guilt. Instead, this part of the process is all about seeing reality for what it truly is. And more than that, it's about seeing ourselves the way God sees us. We are deeply flawed, but despite that, we are deeply loved.

There's a psalm that so perfectly encapsulates the work of Step 4:

> Search me, God, and know my heart;
>   test me and know my anxious thoughts.
> See if there is any offensive way in me,
>   and lead me in the way everlasting.
>
> PSALM 139:23-24, NIV

Pray this passage to begin the work of this chapter.

VIDEO NOTES

As you watch the video, use the space below to take notes. We've included some key points to get you started.

SCAN HERE TO WATCH THE VIDEO FOR STEP 4.

"Search me, God, and know my heart; test me and know my anxious thoughts. See if there is any offensive way in me" (Psalm 139:23-24, NIV).

There is plenty wrong with us.

Step 4 is not something we do with our emotions. What we want here is clarity.

Step 4 must be both fearless and searching.

Why does our inventory have to be fearless? It also has to be searching. Because we are always tempted to let ourselves off the hook.

Our capacity for self-deception is beyond our ability to control.

The good news is, we're already really good at taking inventory. The bad news is, we're good at taking other people's inventory.

We most vividly remember the hurts that we have received, not the hurts that we have inflicted.

A three-step fear inventory can help. Firstly, name your fear honestly. Secondly, is there an action you are being invited to take? Thirdly, ask God for the grace to be present in this moment with him.

Writing it down helps us to see it clearly.

DISCUSSION QUESTIONS

Use these questions to discuss in a small group or reflect individually in your workbook.

1. Have you ever done a moral inventory before? If so, how did it go? How do you feel when you think about doing one now?

2. Do you notice yourself taking *other* people's inventory more easily than your own? If so, why do you think this is?

3. Why do you think we're so prone to self-deception? What's an area in your life where you've noticed this tendency?

4. What's the biggest potential barrier to starting your fearless and searching inventory this week?

KEY ACTIVITIES

Barriers to Entry

Before we can start our fearless and searching moral inventory, it helps to admit that most of us resist it inside. In fact, there are several barriers to entry we might encounter along the way (detailed in *Steps*, 88–93).

- *Whatabout-ism:* We can sometimes talk about people who have hurt us instead of looking at the ways we've hurt others.

- *At least-ism:* We have a tendency to compare ourselves to others we believe are in worse shape than we are.
- *"I don't think I need it":* We fall prey to the fundamental attribution error, where we believe our shortcomings are due to external circumstances outside our control but we attribute other people's mistakes to their character. We lack self-awareness, which by definition means we are not fully aware of what we need.
- *"God can forgive me without it":* We use grace as an excuse not to participate in self-examination.
- *"I've tried it before, and it didn't help":* People often mistake taking inventory for introspection, which isn't the same thing. This one is done with God's help.
- *"It will hurt":* We may falsely believe that if we didn't know the truth, we wouldn't be hurt. Avoidance of pain leads us to stagnation.

Take a moment to consider: Which of these barriers do you most resonate with? Is there a particular item on this list that might interfere with your ability to truly, honestly take part in Step 4?

The Four-Column Inventory

In chapter 4B, John gives us a framework from the Twelve Steps for how to begin taking inventory (*Steps*, 96–97). It requires four columns: Resentment, Event/Cause, My Response, and Where Was I to Blame?

In a moment, we'll begin filling out the inventory. For now, though, revisit the verses from Psalm 139 that we looked at earlier (see page 41). Pray for God to help you search your heart.

On the following page, after taking a deep, centering breath, you can start to fill out your resentment inventory. After you complete each row, pause and thank God for showing you this truth. Ask him to help you come out of hiding and embrace reality with open arms.

Note: This will take many pages. You likely will not have enough space in this workbook to complete the entire inventory. When you run out of rows, simply draw four columns on blank sheets of paper and keep going until you're finished.

John writes, "You may be thinking that if you did this thoroughly, it would take many pages. You would be right. Again, the key people in our lives will have been involved in many resentments, so their names will occur many times" (*Steps*, 98).

Finally, remember that when you take inventory, each item must be concrete and specific. Be fearless. Be searching. Now's a great time to start.

RESENTMENT	EVENT/CAUSE	MY RESPONSE	WHERE WAS I TO BLAME?

Face Your Fears

The fear inventory is "a simple spiritual framework to help people take constructive action in the face of fear" (*Steps*, 100). Naming your fears, maybe counterintuitively, can actually result in great freedom. You will learn a lot about yourself and what drives your behaviors. Like John, you may even experience relief (see *Steps*, 101).

So, now, let's try it together. Take a moment and write three to five fears below. John gives this tip: "Don't allow fear to exist as a vague, unnamed cloud of anxiety. List each fear clearly in simple language" (*Steps*, 102). For example, you might be scared you'll lose a friendship, or maybe you're afraid your marriage is in trouble.

Consider your greatest fears right now, and face them head-on by writing them down:

____

____

____

____

____

Put It into Action

John writes, "Fear, rightly used, is a gift" (*Steps*, 103).

Sometimes fear is actually calling us to take action. John gives this example: "If, when you name your fears, you find yourself writing, 'I am afraid the IRS is going to come after me because I haven't paid my taxes,' then take the second step and pay your taxes. Don't pray, 'God, keep the IRS away'; actually do what you know needs to be done" (*Steps*, 103).

So . . . what needs to be done? Revisit your fear inventory from the previous activity and then jot down some related next-step actions you might need to take.

Abundant Grace

We close this step with the acknowledgment that facing our fears and shortcomings is hard. And it's not a one-and-done process. When we are afraid, we're not called to push through or bury our fear. Instead, the invitation is to take it to God and work through it together.

John writes, "According to Jesus, what is 'fixed' about us—what is established permanently and irrevocably—is not our *talent* but our *worth*. If we believe our talent is fixed and our worth is variable, we'll live in fear. If we believe our worth is fixed and our talent is variable, we'll live in growth" (*Steps*, 106).

Right now, take a moment to ask God for his help to be present and to face the fears in your life. Write down what thoughts or emotions might rise to the surface.

SCRIPTURE FOR REFLECTION

Use this section to reflect on some verses that shed light on this step. You might ask God to reveal what he wants you to take away from them.

> Search me, God, and know my heart;
>   test me and know my anxious thoughts.
> See if there is any offensive way in me,
>   and lead me in the way everlasting.
>
> **PSALM 139:23-24, NIV**

Keep this psalm close throughout this whole journey. Ask God to show you what has been hidden in your heart.

> This is my command—be strong and courageous! Do not be afraid or discouraged. For the LORD your God is with you wherever you go.
>
> **JOSHUA 1:9**

There are so many verses in the Bible where God says not to be afraid. With God's help, maybe we're called to do the very thing we're afraid of. How do you feel about facing your fears? Has anyone in your life ever challenged you to do so?

> If we confess our sins to him, he is faithful and just to forgive us our sins and to cleanse us from all wickedness.
>
> **1 JOHN 1:9**

When you read this verse, remember that confession—bringing our shortcomings into the light—is healing. What healing might you experience through confession?

CLOSING THOUGHTS

Let's recap the journey we've been on together. So far, we've admitted we were powerless over our deepest problems. We've acknowledged that on our own, our life has become unmanageable. Then, we came to believe that a Power greater than ourselves could restore us to sanity. In Step 3, we made a decision to turn our will and our life over to the care of God as we understood him.

Now, in Step 4, we're making a searching and fearless moral inventory of ourselves. This is everything—including the bad and the ugly. The stuff we're normally inclined to sweep under the rug. We do this in pursuit of cold, hard reality.

In this step, we aren't shaming ourselves or succumbing to guilt. Rather, we are owning the areas where we've fallen short and (sometimes for the first time ever) seeing them clearly. John says it this way: "Shame and guilt can make the prospect of this step seem dreadful, so know that there is freedom and peace on the other side. We can hardly remind ourselves enough of Paul's statement that 'Therefore, there is now *no condemnation* for those who are in Christ Jesus.' God is with us to help us" (*Steps*, 93).

As you walk through the inventory exercises, you might notice that maybe it's not as terrifying as you thought it would be. It's an act of receiving grace, standing with arms wide open to God and learning that you are still loved, mistakes and all. So before moving on to the next step, pause and rest here for a moment. Let God's grace wash over you and your life. Ask God for his presence.

And a quick reminder: This step could take a long time. It could take many full notebooks before you're truly able to move on to Step 5.

When you do, get ready. Next up, we're going to step into vulnerability and transparency like never before.

Keep coming back. It works if you work it.

JOURNAL SPACE

After completing this chapter, take five to ten minutes of silence. Then think through these questions in the journaling space that follows:

- What do I sense God saying to me through this material?
- As I inventoried, which aspect(s) felt particularly hard? Was there anything I had to dig deep for?
- What did I learn about myself in this step?

STEP 5

The Confession: Into the Light

We admitted to God, to ourselves, and to another human being the exact nature of our wrongs.

STEPS, PAGES 109–131

OPENING REFLECTION

If Step 4 helps us see ourselves as we truly are, Step 5 allows us to step fully into the light. First we see ourselves clearly, and then we say it out loud.

Something sacred takes place within this step. It brings out our character traits that hide in the darkness and exposes them to the light. It's the moment when what was hidden can be revealed. Great freedom comes with this step.

John puts it this way: "If we are to grow spiritually, our desire to be known and accepted must become greater than our desire to hide and self-protect" (*Steps*, 113). So we come out of hiding . . . together.

In this step, we'll find one person to trust with our sins, wrongdoings, missteps, disappointments, regrets, and character defects. Whatever you uncovered in Step 4 you'll reveal to another soul in Step 5. John calls this person a "*fully disclosing friend*" and discusses his in detail in chapter 5A (see *Steps*, 111–112). This step will help you identify yours and, through this process, unlock great freedom in your life. Time to become known.

Before we go any farther, let's pray:

God, you already know everything about me. You know me inside and out. You know everything I've done, everything I've thought about doing, everything I will do in the future. You know the thoughts I've had, the words I regret. Please reveal through Step 5 that confession isn't shameful; it's a ticket to freedom. I don't have to be afraid. Help me trust that when I reveal my shortcomings to another person, you will use it to form me into someone more like you. You will meet me with more love and more grace than I can imagine. Amen.

VIDEO NOTES

As you watch the video, use the space below to take notes. We've included some key points to get you started.

SCAN HERE TO WATCH THE VIDEO FOR STEP 5.

The next step is "We admitted to God, to ourselves, and to another human being the exact nature of our wrongs."

All of this wisdom comes from Scripture: "Confess your sins to each other and pray for each other so that you may be healed" (James 5:16).

The idea is to look for someone to whom we can be fully disclosing.

We can only be loved to the extent that we are known. We can only be fully loved if we are fully known.

Fill out each quadrant as John names squares in the video:

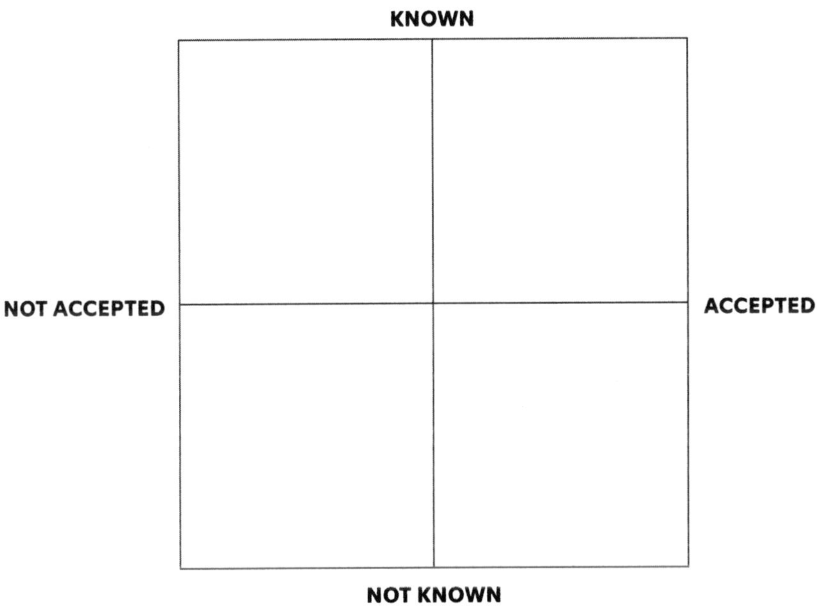

After taking the fifth step in Alcoholics Anonymous, the desire to drink for many people begins to fade, because such deep healing is taking place.

Step 5 is a step whose power and value become clear only after we take it.

DISCUSSION QUESTIONS

Use these questions to discuss in a small group or reflect individually in your workbook.

1. When you consider sharing the ugly or painful parts of yourself, how does it feel? What emotions surface in you as you think about finding a fully disclosing friend?

2. Consider the parameters John gives for suitable candidates for fully disclosing friendships (see *Steps*, 119–123). Has there ever been a time you jumped too quickly into trusting someone in a sensitive capacity? What about a time when you trusted someone with something potentially painful and it paid off for you? What can you learn from these experiences as you choose who to partner with for Step 5?

3. What was your reaction to the story John told in the video about his friend, Dr. Rick, and how he responded after they completed Step 5 together? (You can also read this story in *Steps*, 119.) Have you ever experienced acceptance like this? If not, what do you imagine this acceptance would feel like? What is the link between confession and acceptance?

4. How might completing Step 5 change your view of how God sees you?

KEY ACTIVITIES

The Three Parts of Confession

- *To God:* We confess to our Father because only he can heal the deepest parts of us.
- *To ourselves:* We confess to ourselves because the process begins with self-awareness.
- *To another person:* We confess to someone else because true freedom comes through reliance on community.

Now take a moment to think about each type of confession. Use the table below to plan how you might carry out each one in practice. We've filled in examples to help you get started.

CONFESSION TYPE	MY PLAN
To God . . .	Example: During prayer this week, I'll stop performing. Instead, I will think about one of the ways I've sinned recently and tell God about it honestly.
To God . . .	
To myself . . .	Example: At the end of the day today, I will write down the exact nature of my wrongs over the course of the day and admit where I fell short.
To myself . . .	
To another person . . .	Example: I'll start small by telling a trusted friend one thing I've done wrong.
To another person . . .	

Naming What's Hidden

Take a moment to revisit what you learned in Step 4, when you made your inventory. Now, choose one area or memory that you've never told anyone.

Write a short, honest statement here. No explanations needed; just name it.

God, I need to tell the truth about ______________________.

Now stop and notice how this feels. What comes up? Are you anxious, fearful? Perhaps frustrated?

Often, just naming the truth loosens sin's grip on our life.

Choosing Your Fully Disclosing Friend

As you now know, Step 5 isn't meant to be done alone. When you approach this step, you will need to identify the person you feel safe confiding in. Here are some characteristics to watch for:

- Someone who listens more than they speak
- Someone who offers "non-condemning, non-shaming acceptance" (*Steps*, 119)
- Someone you can deeply trust who will honor confidentiality
- Someone who is a courageous truth-teller (see *Steps*, 121–122 for more on this)

Brainstorm a few names of people in your life who might be good candidates:

Then pray this prayer:

> *God, would you help me choose the right person? Remind me that you've already gone before me, that you hold the future, and that confession will lead me farther into your freedom. Amen.*

Reframing the Question

On page 125 in *Steps*, John shares this quote: "Many of us grew up basing our decision on: 'Do I want to do this or not?'" John observes, "The question that matters is: 'What do I *need* to do if I truly want to grow?'"

Consider your heart posture regarding Step 5 for a moment. Use the prompts below to answer honestly whether there's a gap between what you want and what you need on this journey.

What I want to do: ______________________________

____

____

What I need to do: ______________________________

____

____

What God might be growing within me: ______________________________

____

____

Grace to the Fullest

In chapter 5C, we learn about what's called "doorknob disclosures" (*Steps*, 127). John describes this phenomenon as a sensational admission made to a therapist in the last few moments of a patient's session. In other words, we often put off the thing we know we most need to say. (Why do we do this?!)

John puts it this way: "What should you talk about? One good rule of thumb is to start with what you most don't want to talk about" (*Steps*, 127).

So, let's give it a shot. Think for a few minutes about the thing you are most tempted to hide, to bury, to conceal. Then write it down. You don't have to go into detail; just admit to yourself within this workbook what topic you're most hesitant to reveal. Then let God reassure you that it's a good thing to share.

SCRIPTURE FOR REFLECTION

Use this section to reflect on some verses that shed light on this step. You might ask God to reveal what he wants you to take away from them.

> Confess your sins to each other and pray for each other so that you may be healed. The earnest prayer of a righteous person has great power and produces wonderful results.
>
> **JAMES 5:16**

James knows the power of confession. Think about what it could mean in your life too.

> Oh, what joy for those
>   whose disobedience is forgiven,
>   whose sin is put out of sight!
> Yes, what joy for those
>   whose record the LORD has cleared of guilt,
>   whose lives are lived in complete honesty!
>
> **PSALM 32:1-2**

Your sins are fully covered. What does that mean for you? How often do you consider the gravity of God having redefined your life on the cross?

> If we are living in the light, as God is in the light, then we have fellowship with each other, and the blood of Jesus, his Son, cleanses us from all sin.
>
> **1 JOHN 1:7**

Is there a part of your story that God is inviting you to bring into the light?

CLOSING THOUGHTS

Congratulations on making it to the end of Step 5! This step isn't easy (are any of them, really?), as it's the first outward step. Up to this point, everything has been purely between you and God. The first four steps are internal, but Step 5 requires real humility and vulnerability with another person to move forward. As we confess, we may be tempted to soften our actions, to skip what feels humiliating, to hide what feels shameful. But the power in this step comes from *full* disclosure. And with God's help, you can do it.

What usually follows is surprising to most people. They experience a deeper sense of belonging, a lightness of spirit, and the beginning of a transformation unlike anything they've ever felt before.

In fact, many people in AA find that Step 5 is when they lose the desire to drink altogether. It's the hardest step to start, but the freedom on the other side is greater than you can imagine. When someone hears your story and chooses to accept you in spite of it, something inside you begins to believe that God will too.

And then, when you're ready, Step 6 will help you begin turning that healing into lasting change.

Keep coming back. There's more freedom ahead.

JOURNAL SPACE

After completing this chapter, take five to ten minutes of silence. Then think through these questions in the journaling space that follows:

- What truth do I most need to say to someone else?
- What aspects of this step am I most afraid of?
- What could freedom look like for me on the other side of this step?

STEP 6

The Preparation: Became Entirely Ready

We were entirely ready to have God remove all these defects of character.

STEPS, PAGES 133–154

OPENING REFLECTION

"Now, having recognized my own powerlessness but also God's strength, having surrendered my life and will and honestly examined my character and humbled myself by admitting all this to not only God and myself but also another person—*now* I'm ready to change" (*Steps*, 135).

Such a beautiful summary of the journey so far. Except . . . there are still parts of us that definitely *aren't* ready to change. The part that fears boredom with the "new me." The part that feels afraid, or anxious, or uncertain about the future.

John says it this way: "I'm ready. Pretty ready. When I'm in the right mood, or at church, or got caught doing something embarrassing. I'm just not *entirely* ready" (*Steps*, 135). Get the gist here? The gap between "almost ready" and "entirely ready" is actually mountainous. And Step 6 bridges that gap.

Despite our double-mindedness and cognitive dissonance gone wild, becoming entirely ready for God to remove all our character defects is within reach. This step holds two distinct practices that will get us there. We're going to (1) honestly look at our excuses and (2) get sick and tired of being sick and tired (see *Steps*, 137–140).

This is the step where we stand before God and say, "I'm ready. Change whatever needs changing."

So, are you *entirely ready* to begin? You can do this.

Before we move farther, let's pause and pray:

God, would you help us to move from partially ready to entirely ready? With our whole mind, body, and spirit, would you help to enact real change? Help us to fully surrender, to push past that which holds us back from turning our life completely over to you. Amen.

VIDEO NOTES

As you watch the video, use the space below to take notes. We've included some key points to get you started.

SCAN HERE TO WATCH THE VIDEO FOR STEP 6.

Step 6 is about becoming entirely ready for God to remove our defects of character.

Like all the other steps, this one comes right out of Scripture. Psalm 51 says, "Cleanse me with hyssop, and I will be clean; wash me, and I will be whiter than snow. . . . Create in me a pure heart, O God, and renew a steadfast spirit within me" (verses 7, 10, NIV).

After walking through Step 4 and then talking about that with God, ourselves, and one other person in Step 5, we now have a clearer picture of what our character defects are.

We are ready to change. Except for the part of us that is not.

In this step, we are moving from being almost ready to have God remove our character defects to being entirely ready.

Can you name your primary defects of character? Here are some possibilities:

- Resentment
- Anger
- Fear
- Cowardice
- Self-pity
- Self-justification
- Self-importance
- Egotism
- Self-condemnation
- Guilt
- Lying
- Evasiveness
- Dishonesty
- Impatience
- Hate
- False pride
- Denial
- Jealousy
- Envy
- Laziness
- Procrastination
- Insincerity
- Negative thinking
- Immoral thinking
- Perfectionism
- Criticizing
- Gossip
- Greed

Do a cost-benefit analysis, and for any of those defects of character you named, ask yourself, *What's the advantage? And what's the disadvantage?*

If you're not entirely ready yet, it's because there's something you get out of this defect of character.

DISCUSSION QUESTIONS

Use these questions to discuss in a small group or reflect individually in your workbook.

1. Where would you rate yourself on being "entirely ready," on a scale of 1–10? What factors play into your rating?

2. As John mentioned in the video, we can grow attached to our character traits, whether good or bad. Are there any defects you might have grown attached to or feel afraid to let go of? Why might that be?

3. Why do you think it's so hard to believe that God can actually, *truly* change us?

4. What patterns or habits does your heart secretly want to hang on to?

5. This week, what's one practical way you could practice readiness?

KEY ACTIVITIES

My Go-To Excuses

John suggests that "naming our resistance brings great change" (*Steps*, 140). Take a few minutes to think through your regular Rolodex of excuses. Consider how you are most tempted to excuse your actions. Are you most tempted at work? Perhaps at home? With your kids or spouse? Get honest with yourself now and fill out the table below.

MY TEMPTATIONS	MY EXCUSES	MY MOTIVATIONS

As we've learned, this step is about becoming entirely ready for God to remove our character defects, so take a moment to pray over the table you just completed: *God, help me to become ready with my whole heart to stop using these excuses in my life. I can't, but you can. Amen.*

Constructive Habits

God rarely removes a defect without inviting us to practice something new, something better in its place. In chapter 6B, John provides a guide for adding constructive habits to our life. He writes, "How do habitual character defects get removed? Mostly by getting replaced with newer and better ones. Charles Duhigg notes that 'habits never really disappear.' . . . But change lies in what he calls the 'Golden Rule of Habit Formation': it is exponentially easier to *replace* a habit than to *extinguish* it" (*Steps*, 144).

Go back and reference the character defect list from the video notes section of this step (page 66). Choose one item from your list and walk through the prompts below.

The character defect I'm working on is ____.

What constructive habit might God be inviting me into in place of this defect? You can circle one of these examples or write your own in the lines below.

- Anger → stop and take an intentional pause
- Jealousy → write a gratitude list for all the blessings in my life
- Gossip → say something kind
- Control → ask an open-ended question instead
- Perfectionism → "good enough" completion

Finally, consider: What would happen if I were to develop this habit over time?

Remember, this is not yet about doing things differently—only becoming willing.

What I'm Holding On To

One of the truths just below the surface of Step 6 is that we secretly kind of like our character defects. We enjoy them. They're part of us. The truth is, there's some benefit we're receiving from these behaviors and patterns. They protect us, or numb us, or make us feel powerful. They make us feel joy, or they keep us from feeling pain. Until we're honest about the root cause, we'll never be entirely ready to let them go.

Again, reference your list from Step 4. Choose one defect and work through these prompts.

The character defect I'm examining is ______________________________
____.

The benefit I receive from this defect is ______________________________
______________________________ (e.g., comfort, control, attention, escape).

What does this defect cost me?

If I'm honest, do I want God to remove it completely, or only enough to reduce the consequences?

If you'd like to repeat this exercise on multiple defects, you can use the journal space at the end of this chapter to do so. The point isn't self-condemnation but to let God reveal where you may still be hanging on to old and harmful patterns.

The Readiness Scale

Now it's time to check in with yourself on your readiness in several dimensions of life. Remember, some parts of you will be more ready than others, and that's totally normal. Try to withhold judgment as you consider your scoring. This is about awareness, not shame.

Below are different areas of life where God may be inviting change. You can rate your current readiness in each category using this scale:

1—Not ready at all
2—Slightly willing
3—Somewhat willing
4—Mostly willing
5—Entirely ready

My Relationships (*How open am I to God removing defects that affect the people closest to me?*)

Rating: ____/5

My Work or School Life (*How willing am I to have God transform my habits, attitude, integrity, or ego here?*)

Rating: ____/5

My Finances (*How ready am I for God to form generosity or discipline in my finances?*)

Rating: ____/5

My Emotional Life (*How ready am I for God to reshape patterns like anger, fear, avoidance, envy, or resentment?*)

Rating: ____/5

My Thought Life (*Am I open to God retraining what I think about, how I speak to myself, or the stories from the past that I cling to in the present?*)

Rating: ____/5

My Habits (*How ready am I for God to work on the daily behaviors that quietly shape who I'm becoming?*)

Rating: ____/5

My Sexuality (*How willing am I to let God shape my desires, patterns, boundaries, habits, and the way I relate to my own body and others?*)

Rating: ____/5

My Addictive Patterns (*How ready am I for God to transform the behaviors, substances, screens, habits, or escapes that numb me, soothe me, or help me avoid pain?*)

Rating: ____/5

Take a moment to reflect. There are likely many categories in your life that weren't named above, but it's a great starting point. What did you learn about yourself? Which rating surprises you?

Which areas did you learn are places where you still might not be entirely ready? Write down any thoughts you might have about that.

The Three Lies

In the closing of chapter 6C, John unpacks three illusions, originally identified by Henri Nouwen, that shape our self-worth and drive many of our defects:

1. I am what I have
2. I am what other people think about me
3. I am what I do

These lies fuel compulsions, shame, comparison, and the deep need to prove ourselves. Step 6 invites us to become willing to let God dismantle these inner narratives so we can build our identity somewhere stronger—in him.

Reflect on each of the statements below:

1. "I AM WHAT I HAVE."

How does this show up in your life? (Possessions, status, lifestyle, appearance, achievements, security.)

2. "I AM WHAT OTHER PEOPLE THINK ABOUT ME."

Whose approval (or disapproval) has too much power over your inner world?

3. "I AM WHAT I DO."

Where does performance drive your sense of worth? When do you feel like you're "not enough"?

Now, consider who God says you are. Fill out the blanks with the truth.

In Christ . . .

- I am not what I have. I am ______________________________.
- I am not what others think. I am ________________________.
- I am not what I do. I am _________________________________.

Sit quietly for a moment and let these truths draw you into readiness. Close with this short prayer:

> *God, help me become entirely ready to lay down the false stories I've lived under so I can receive the identity you've already given me. Make me willing to be transformed. Amen.*

SCRIPTURE FOR REFLECTION

Use this section to reflect on some verses that shed light on this step. You might ask God to reveal what he wants you to take away from them.

> I will give you a new heart, and I will put a new spirit in you. I will take out your stony, stubborn heart and give you a tender, responsive heart.
> **EZEKIEL 36:26**

First, isn't it amazing how the Twelve Steps are scripturally supported? You can find guidance in the Bible to back up each part of the process, including Step 6. In this verse, God says he will give you a new heart and put a new spirit in you. What would it mean if God changed your heart today?

> I am certain that God, who began the good work within you, will continue his work until it is finally finished on the day when Christ Jesus returns.
> **PHILIPPIANS 1:6**

How might this verse build trust in you that God can and will change your life?

> Create in me a clean heart, O God.
> Renew a loyal spirit within me.
> **PSALM 51:10**

Use this verse as a prayer. Pray it slowly to God, inviting him to renew a loyal spirit in you.

CLOSING THOUGHTS

This journey started with powerlessness. We came to believe that God could restore us. We turned our will and our life over to his care. We faced the truth head-on and confessed it to another person. We stepped into the freedom on the other side.

Now, we stand here, openhanded. Ready—*entirely* ready—for God to change us.

Step 6 is a posture step. It's a last-10-percent step. The thing about readiness is that it comes in layers. Some parts peel open easily. Others, not so much. Our goal here isn't perfect willingness, but it's to stay close to God, who can create that in us. He will nudge us when there's another layer of readiness that needs to open up.

So right now, take a deep breath. Open your palms to heaven and let go of control. Say with your whole heart (and perhaps even out loud), "God, I'm ready."

Next up is Step 7, where we will meet humility face-to-face.

Keep coming back. God's not done with you yet.

JOURNAL SPACE

After completing this chapter, take five to ten minutes of silence. Then think through these questions in the journaling space on the following page:

- What part of my life am I ready for God to change?
- Is there a part of me that I'm not ready to let go of yet? How might I move toward willingness in that area?
- What could it look like to trust God with both of these things?
- Did you need more space for the "What I'm Holding On To" exercise on pages 71–72? You can use the journaling space for that purpose.

STEP 7

The Petition: Humble Asking

We humbly asked Him to remove our shortcomings.

STEPS, PAGES 155–175

OPENING REFLECTION

Let's review where we've been and where we find ourselves today. In the last several steps, we named our shortcomings and confessed them to ourselves, God, and another person. Then we moved from being *almost* ready to becoming *entirely* ready for God to change us.

Now is our moment. Step 7 is when we finally ask God to do it.

This step marks a shift from self-effort to true, real dependence on God. We can't change alone. We need him to change us. We're moving from *trying harder* to *asking God*. We can't grit our teeth into holiness or will ourselves into healing. We have to admit that we can't remove our character defects alone and ask God to do what only *he* can do.

Humility is simply living in reality. John writes, "God can work with a humble spirit because it is open to him. He cannot work with a proud spirit because it resists him" (*Steps*, 160). This step is postured not in self-hatred or shrinking ourselves down but rather in seeing ourselves truthfully and noticing our strengths, our limitations, and ultimately our deep need for grace.

Step 7 is the honest moment when we stand before God and ask him to change us. Deep breaths—good things are coming.

So now, before we begin Step 7, let's pause together and pray:

God, I ask you to do what I can't do for myself or on my own. Please remove the parts of me that are broken. I'm becoming ready for you to take them away. Get rid of these patterns in my life that you know aren't serving me or bringing me closer to you. I trust you with everything. Amen.

VIDEO NOTES

As you watch the video, use the space below to take notes. We've included some key points to get you started.

SCAN HERE TO WATCH THE VIDEO FOR STEP 7.

Step 7 is the step of asking. We humbly ask God to remove our shortcomings.

The biblical term for God removing our shortcomings is *sanctification*.

To humbly ask means we are not passive. There is a role for us to play.

Our permission, engagement, and participation are deep parts of God honoring personhood.

Step 7 is changing us at the level of habit, transformation of habit.

Drop the rock.

DISCUSSION QUESTIONS

Use these questions to discuss in a small group or reflect individually in your workbook.

1. How does John's definition of humility, "living in reality," expand or challenge your thinking?

2. Where do you see pride show up most often in your life or habits? What does it try to protect?

3. Think for a moment about a shortcoming that continues to resurface. What could it look like to ask God for help removing it?

4. Which area of your life most needs the Step 7 prayer today ("God remove this; I can't do it alone")?

5. Bonus zoom-out question, since you're over the halfway mark: Which step has been hardest for you so far? Why might that be?

KEY ACTIVITIES

Moving Toward Humility

This step is all about building on the six prior to it and asking God for help. John writes, "Asking by its nature is a humbling thing. We don't insist, demand, or dictate. We submit a request. 'God, would you?'" (*Steps*, 158).

The great (and terrifying) news is that we aren't in charge. It's not up to us whether God grants our requests. We don't get to plan the timing or the circumstances or the "how." We just lift our request up in humility and trust him with the rest.

Of course, this means that before we can take on Step 7, we have to have humility. And this activity will help us get there.

Dallas Willard said it this way: "God will gladly give humility to us if, trusting and waiting on him to act, we refrain from *pretending* we are what we know we are not, from *presuming* a favorable position for ourselves and from *pushing* or trying to override the will of others" (quoted in *Steps*, 160–161).

Write down the "three P's" for memory's sake here:

1. ______________________
2. ______________________
3. ______________________

Since humility is such a critical part of this step, we'll spend the next several activities working with the three P's. Ready? Onward.

Pretending

How often do we pretend to be better than we are? We put up a front, letting people think things we know aren't true.

John challenges us on this: "No saying, 'I've read that book' when you haven't; 'I know that person' when you don't; 'I accomplished this' when you didn't; 'I'm this smart/liked/strong/competent' when you're not" (*Steps*, 161).

So, in this activity, take a moment to consider where in your life you most often pretend. Examples might include saying, "I'm fine," when you're really not. Or acting like you have it all together, even when you're falling apart on the inside. Think about it and then jot down an example or two below.

Area(s) Where I Pretend:

Now, consider this: What might you be afraid of happening if you were honest in this area?

Presuming

This world is full of presumption. Have you ever heard the phrase, "We judge others by their actions and ourselves by our intentions"? So often (and as we learned in Step 4!), we jump to conclusions about people around us while excusing away our own flaws.

When thinking about presuming, John writes, "No entitlement. No expectations about being treated as though you're top chicken in the pecking order. No concern about being seated at the head table. No mansplaining. Appreciate waitstaff. Give up a good parking space. Learn from someone else's ethnicity or religion. Don't assume bad motives" (*Steps*, 161).

Now take a moment to think about an area where you're likely to presume. Maybe you think you already know enough about someone or something. Maybe you jump to the worst explanation when something worrying happens. Write down what comes to mind.

Area(s) Where I Presume:

What if I approached my life with curiosity instead of certainty?

Pushing

The third P is pushing. It's that inner force that tries to white-knuckle change into our life. It's effortful, strained, and all willpower.

But that's not surrender.

This kind of posture promotes burnout and discouragement. So we work to remove it.

John distills it this way: "No self-promoting. Take the day off from building your brand. Listen. Work well. Help out. Let someone else at the meeting talk first. Deflect credit. Get the coffee. Run the errand" (*Steps*, 161).

Think about the areas you most try to control. Are you approaching burnout in any aspect of your life? Are you holding tightly to something God meant for you to trust him with? Complete the activities below to help you identify these areas.

Area(s) Where I Push in My Life:

What would it look like to make the shift between pushing by my own strength and receiving from God in his?

Three P's Reflection

Again, humbly presenting our requests to God requires humility. It's right there in the step! So now that we've worked on Dallas Willard's "three P's," let's pause to consider which of them may lead the way in your life. What pattern laid out above do you struggle with most? What do you gravitate toward when it comes to ego? And how might this habit be reflected even in your relationship with God?

Between pretending, presuming, and pushing, I am most apt to

______________________________.

How does this tendency show up in how I relate to God?

How could humility grow in my life if I were to set aside this pattern?

OWN, Don't Enthrone

In chapter 7A, we were thinking about how to build humility in such a way as to be able to approach God with our requests. But in 7B, John reminds us that while we're asking God to remove our defects, we are not passive. He writes, "A helpful way to navigate troubling emotions comes from my psychologist friend Rick: OWN them, don't *enthrone* them. Emotions are good servants but bad masters. So each time I ask God for help, the little acronym OWN involves three actions" (*Steps*, 164).

Read through the quick explanation for each one and then complete the activity below.

- *Observe:* "I ask God's help to become the world's leading expert at noticing what's going on in my mind. I learn to have thoughts and feelings without allowing them to have me. Only God has me" (*Steps*, 164).

- *Welcome:* Rather than resisting negative emotions, we *welcome* them. This one can feel paradoxical. "We empower negative emotions when we try to resist them. It's like trying to hold an inflated beach ball underwater. Eventually we will get tired of holding it down. The ball is very patient. It knows it will win in the end. What we resist, persists" (*Steps*, 165–166).
- *Name:* "When we name a negative emotion, we identify it for what it is—simply a thought or desire we are experiencing that is temporary. It will pass, it is not to be identified with 'reality,' and it does not have to sit on the throne of our life" (*Steps*, 167).

So now, let's practice OWNing. John has a few suggestions on page 168 of *Steps*. Maybe you could sit in stillness for five to ten minutes and simply notice what sensations surface within your body. Are you tense? Worried? Stressed? Clenched?

Another way you can practice this is sitting in the quiet to simply listen to the voice in your head. It never stops. What does it talk about? You could write down, nonjudgmentally, some of the things it says.

Choose an exercise and journal about what you learn.

Drop the Rock

Brace yourself for some frustrating news: Even if we master Step 7 today, we still have to go back into the real world. We still have to face the many, many irritants of reality, the well-worn ruts of annoyance in our neural pathways. "The stress around us will trigger the weaknesses within us. And often we won't even recognize it" (*Steps*, 170).

In chapter 7C, John compares our character defects to a heavy rock we cling to while trying to swim. We kick harder. We strain more. We eventually get exhausted. All the while, the real problem is actually the weight in our hands—the thing we, ourselves, are carrying.

Step 7 invites a simple shift: stop trying harder and gently let the rock go.

We'll close by taking a quiet moment to answer one question: What's the "rock" you're still carrying that God is inviting you to release?

Now, open your hands, if you'd like, and pray this prayer:

> *God, this has weighed me down long enough. I can't drop it on my own. I'm willing to receive your help. Help me let it go. Remove what I cannot remove myself. Amen.*

SCRIPTURE FOR REFLECTION

Use this section to reflect on some verses that shed light on this step. You might ask God to reveal what he wants you to take away from them.

> He leads the humble in doing right,
> teaching them his way.
>
> **PSALM 25:9**

How does this encourage you to ask for help in your life?

> [God] gives grace generously. As the Scriptures say,
>
> "God opposes the proud
> but gives grace to the humble."
>
> **JAMES 4:6**

How might this verse highlight the path toward grace for you today?

> I am certain that God, who began the good work within you, will continue his work until it is finally finished on the day when Christ Jesus returns.
>
> **PHILIPPIANS 1:6**

Consider this truth: God is the one removing shortcomings. Not you. (See Steps 1–3.) Do you ever get this mixed up in your mind and heart?

CLOSING THOUGHTS

Step 7 is a moment when real spiritual change begins to take root. We've walked through truth-telling, readiness, inventory, and confession, and Step 7 brings us to a powerful prayer: "God, I humbly ask you to remove my shortcomings."

At this stage, something tender often happens inside us. We begin to notice the habits that keep us stuck. We see ourselves clearly. We see the ways we've been pretending, holding up an image of strength we don't actually possess. We notice where we've been presuming, assuming we already know enough or that we're not the problem. We even catch ourselves pushing, trying to change through strain and willpower rather than grace.

Step 7 gently disarms all of that. Humility says, *I am done pretending. I don't have to presume. I don't need to push.*

I can just ask.

John also gives us two other pillars that shape this step:

- *OWN, don't enthrone:* We own our shortcomings with honesty, but they don't have the final word.
- *Drop the rock:* We learned about the drop-the-rock parable. Clinging to our old patterns is like swimming with a boulder in our arms. Step 7 is the moment we loosen our grip and drop the rock.

And here's the relief: You don't have to remove anything yourself. You don't have to try harder.

Your only job is to be humble and honest as you invite God into the places you can't fix on your own. So rest for a moment. You've told the truth. You've opened your hands. Now let God do the part only *he* can do.

When you're ready, Step 8 will turn this newfound freedom outward into relationships, amends, courage, and repair. But you don't need to be there yet.

For now, just take a deep breath. Ask humbly. Release freely.

And keep coming back. It works if you work it.

JOURNAL SPACE

After completing this chapter, take five to ten minutes of silence. Then think through these questions in the journaling space that follows:

- Now that you've moved past Step 6 and studied Step 7, do you feel entirely ready to ask God to remove your shortcomings? Why or why not?
- What concrete next step will you take this week?

STEP 8

The Damage: Named Those We've Harmed

We made a list of all persons we had harmed and became willing to make amends to them all.

STEPS, PAGES 177–200

OPENING REFLECTION

The first seven steps have mostly been internal work. Honesty. Confession. Humility. Reflection. We've been learning how to tell the truth about ourselves and let God reshape us.

In Step 8, though, something begins to change. The focus starts to move beyond us. God is beginning to form us and to impact those around us.

This matters a lot in a world marked by anger and resentment. As John says in chapter 8A, "We live in what is sometimes called the age of rage" (*Steps*, 179). The internet abounds with posts and comments at which to get mad. The world seems filled with anger but offers us very little wisdom about what, exactly, we should do with it. So we often "carry our indignation along with us and look for someone to discharge it on" (*Steps*, 179).

Against that backdrop, Scripture gives us a different picture to consider. In *Steps*, we're invited to consider the story of Zacchaeus in Luke 19. When Zacchaeus meets Jesus, something shifts in his life. Zacchaeus gets a new kind of clarity. His old ways of hurting people don't seem so compelling anymore. John puts it this way: "He realizes he cannot be in a relationship of love with Jesus and continue to harm the people around him" (*Steps*, 184).

This is one of the miracles in this journey. As love and humility take root in our life, there's simply less room for bitterness and grudges, less energy for

Facebook comment wars. John captures this transformation as he reflects on Zacchaeus's story:

> Zacchaeus's heart is so overwhelmed with love that his old list—who despises his work, who mocks his body, who envies his wealth—*that* list is gone.
>
> Now he has a new list: those he has harmed. "This widow, these children, that elderly person, those beggars . . . for the sake of this possibility of life I have found through my new friend Jesus, I am now willing to make amends." (*Steps*, 184)

This is the heart of Step 8. It's work worth doing. Step 8 won't be easy, but it will be worth it—that's for sure.

Before we move farther into this step, let's pause and pray:

> *Lord, give me courage to see things as they are. Give me humility to take responsibility for my actions. And, please, give me grace to become willing. Show me where I've hurt people, where relationships are broken, and prepare my heart to make them right. Make me ready, freely and fully. Amen.*

VIDEO NOTES

As you watch the video, use the space below to take notes. We've included some key points to get you started.

SCAN HERE TO WATCH THE VIDEO FOR STEP 8.

Step 8 is a pivotal moment. Up to now, the steps have focused primarily on our character and our relationship with God. In this step, we move from the vertical dimension to the horizontal dimension of life—the people we have harmed.

This step begins with making a list. We can choose to keep a list of people who have harmed us, or we can make a list of the people we have harmed. We make this list not to beat ourselves up or to live in guilt but because love wants to make things right.

We are responsible for cleaning up our side of the street, not managing or judging the other person's response. This step is about our actions, not theirs.

The list you write down should include:

- The name of each person you have harmed
- The exact nature of the harm (specific actions, not vague or defensive apologies)
- The character defect that contributed to the harm

Pray for the willingness to make amends to all the people you have harmed. Willingness is so central that it requires its own step.

Zacchaeus is a picture of Step 8.

We cannot make ourselves willing, but we can sincerely pray for willingness.

Step 8 is simple and doable. Make the list. Pray for willingness.

DISCUSSION QUESTIONS

Use these questions to discuss in a small group or reflect individually in your workbook.

1. Just like the progression from Steps 6 to 7, we're first becoming willing here. Step 8 isn't about the actual repair, not yet. It's about posturing our heart in such a way that we will be ready to reach out to those we've hurt. What parts of your heart don't feel willing yet?

2. John writes, "Mismanaged anger is enemy number one" (*Steps*, 181). How have you seen this concept play out in your world?

3. When you think about the story of Zacchaeus, what parts specifically stand out? Do you relate to him in any particular way?

4. Is there a relationship that comes to mind in dread when you consider having to repair or make amends? What might God be surfacing there?

5. What about your life would look different if you replaced avoidance with willingness?

KEY ACTIVITIES

Make Your List

Step 8 calls us to action: Make a list of all the people we have harmed. Talk about a homework assignment.

It's important to keep in mind that this is not a list to punish ourselves or relive our past. It is a list that will help surface honesty and healing. It is our Zacchaeus moment—the beginning of turning toward repair.

To help guide you, here is the wisdom John offers in chapter 8B regarding what this list should include (see *Steps*, 192).

For each person you've harmed, write down:

- Their name.
- The specific action or incident where you caused harm. Be concrete. Vague apologies hide the truth.
- The character flaw behind the harm (be it greed, envy, deception, impatience, self-righteousness, bitterness, apathy, pride, vanity, sloth, grandiosity, etc.).
- Your current level of willingness to make amends (Yes/No/Maybe).

Here are a few things to remember:

- If you've harmed someone multiple times, list each incident separately.
- If you're not sure someone belongs on your list, put them on anyway.
- If you don't know where they are today, that doesn't matter. The point right now is honesty, not logistics.
- And yes, this could be a long process. It might take days or even weeks. That's okay.

You may wonder what to do if you don't want to write someone's name down. You're not alone. Often the following thoughts can surface during this exercise (see *Steps*, 186–191):

- *They hurt me more than I hurt them.*
- *They don't deserve forgiveness.*

- *I don't know where they are.*
- *This is going to take forever.*

John has a response to this. You are only responsible for *your own* house, not other people's. This step is not about who deserves what. It's about becoming the kind of person who can fully walk in truth and love. (See *Steps*, 187.)

So now, take a few minutes to begin. If you need more space (and you likely will), the journal pages at the end of this chapter are available to continue writing.

PEOPLE I HAVE HARMED:

1. Name: ____________________
   Action: ______________________________________
   Character flaw: ______________________________
   Willingness: Yes / No / Maybe

2. Name: ____________________
   Action: ______________________________________
   Character flaw: ______________________________
   Willingness: Yes / No / Maybe

3. Name: ____________________
   Action: ______________________________________
   Character flaw: ______________________________
   Willingness: Yes / No / Maybe

4. Name: ____________________
   Action: ______________________________________
   Character flaw: ______________________________
   Willingness: Yes / No / Maybe

(Continue as needed in the journal pages or elsewhere.)

Barriers to Willingness

As we saw in the first activity, there are some barriers that can get in our way when it comes to a willingness to make amends. Read through the barriers listed below and then take a moment to reflect.

- "They don't deserve it."
- "It would be too humiliating."
- "God will forgive me without it."
- "I couldn't afford it."
- "I don't want to."
- "I can't think of anyone I've harmed."

Which of the above do you recognize in your life? Circle the barrier that rises to the top for you. In a few sentences, describe how you've seen this barrier take shape.

Finally, ask yourself this question: What would willingness in this area look like for me?

Counting the Cost

Chapter 8C in *Steps* is all about forgiveness. But in order to forgive, we have to move past our resentment and hurt. Counting the cost of holding on to them can be a helpful part of this journey. Consider what it's costing you to continue living wounded.

So right now, think of one person you need to forgive. Then, answer the questions below.

How has holding on to resentment toward this person shaped my life or affected me?

What emotional or spiritual real estate does this take up in my life? (For example, "I spend a lot of time thinking about this," or "I'm not able to pray as effectively because I'm angry.")

Finally, what might change inside me if I released even a little of the resentment I feel?

Expressive Writing

Sometimes a pain or trauma can live so deeply within us that we cannot fathom how to move past it. One way to approach this is through expressive writing. On page 199 of *Steps*, John suggests focusing on a traumatic event or season that causes you the greatest pain. He says, "Get a journal, and for twenty minutes write without filter or self-censoring directly about these events."

Focus particularly on your emotional responses to them. What did you feel and think?

Keep in mind that this activity is meant to help you prepare for willingness, not excuse or avoid making amends. Note: If this particular exercise is too painful for you, you can opt to seek help from a licensed mental health professional to discuss instead.

Set a timer and start writing. When your twenty minutes is up, stop, reflect, rest, and pray the prayer at the end of these journaling pages.

Reflect for a few moments and then pray this prayer:

> *God, please take what surfaced here and create willingness in my heart. Help me see the truth of what I have done wrong and what others have done wrong. Help me see others as you do and give me courage to take the steps I need to take. Amen.*

SCRIPTURE FOR REFLECTION

Use this section to reflect on some verses that shed light on this step. You might ask God to reveal what he wants you to take away from them.

> Jesus entered Jericho and made his way through the town. There was a man there named Zacchaeus. He was the chief tax collector in the region, and he had become very rich. He tried to get a look at Jesus, but he was too short to see over the crowd. So he ran ahead and climbed a sycamore-fig tree beside the road, for Jesus was going to pass that way.
>
> When Jesus came by, he looked up at Zacchaeus and called him by name. "Zacchaeus!" he said. "Quick, come down! I must be a guest in your home today."
>
> Zacchaeus quickly climbed down and took Jesus to his house in great excitement and joy. But the people were displeased. "He has gone to be the guest of a notorious sinner," they grumbled.
>
> Meanwhile, Zacchaeus stood before the Lord and said, "I will give half my wealth to the poor, Lord, and if I have cheated people on their taxes, I will give them back four times as much!"
>
> Jesus responded, "Salvation has come to this home today, for this man has shown himself to be a true son of Abraham. For the Son of Man came to seek and save those who are lost."
>
> **LUKE 19:1-10**

How does Zacchaeus's transformation speak to your own desire to make things right?

> Do all that you can to live in peace with everyone.
>
> **ROMANS 12:18**

Is there someone you avoid because it feels too complicated to pursue repair? How does this verse speak to that?

> If you are presenting a sacrifice at the altar in the Temple and you suddenly remember that someone has something against you, leave your sacrifice there at the altar. Go and be reconciled to that person. Then come and offer your sacrifice to God.
>
> **MATTHEW 5:23-24**

Why might Jesus tie worship and reconciliation together in the same thought?

CLOSING THOUGHTS

In Step 8, you gain a type of clarity you can get only through humility and love, and only with God's help. You realize there has been impact because of your actions. There are people who have been hurt along the way.

In this step, we stop excusing. Stop minimizing. Stop explaining. We put aside image management and mental gymnastics, self-protection and hiding. Sometimes the amount of pain we've carried from prior relationships makes the mere idea of repair feel overwhelming or even impossible, but it's not. With the work from Steps 1 through 7, you can do this.

And the good news is, we aren't contacting anyone right now. Not yet.

Right now, your job isn't to be fully ready to establish contact. For the moment, all you have to be is *willing to become willing*.

So don't rush. Don't force it. Just keep showing up, keep admitting where you were wrong, keep praying for humility, keep opening your palms to heaven.

And when you're ready, Step 9 will help translate this willingness into action. For now, though, let Step 8 soften your heart.

Keep coming back. It works if you work it.

JOURNAL SPACE

After completing this chapter, take five to ten minutes of silence. Then think through these questions in the journaling space that follows:

- Pulse check: How am I feeling about the Twelve Steps and my progress so far?
- What is God revealing in my heart through Step 8?
- What is one next step I can take right now?

STEP 9

The Reparation: Made Amends

We made direct amends to such people wherever possible, except when to do so would injure them or others.

STEPS, PAGES 201–222

OPENING REFLECTION

By the time we reach Step 9, we've looked at our life through a new lens, naming people we've harmed, facing realities we once avoided, and stepping directly into that which may cause us pain. Most recently, we've asked God to grow our willingness, as we've done throughout the entire process.

Now, Step 9 asks us to approach the people we've hurt and make it right. Needless to say, this one requires great courage.

John puts it this way: "We must engage in a countercultural activity. We must learn to blame ourselves. We must dare to be guilty. We must discover the awesome, liberating power of contrition" (*Steps*, 217). *Dare to be guilty.* That's an unpopular concept nowadays. It's one we will face head-on in this step.

First, though, it's important to be clear about a few things. To start, we aren't doing this to relieve our own guilt or "get something off our chest." That would make it about *us*. This step is about righting wrongs for the sake of the other person and the person we're becoming. Making amends is for repairing relationships, and it is the relational fruit of the spiritual work we've done in the last eight steps.

Second, making amends doesn't guarantee reconciliation. Those are two different things. We are only responsible for ourselves, not how the other person responds. We are to be faithful, not forceful. The goal is repair, not resolution on the exact terms we want.

Third, "direct amends wherever possible" doesn't mean at all costs. Love and wisdom and nuance matter a lot here (see *Steps*, 205–206, for more on this). In some situations, direct contact would cause great harm, and that's not what this step is about. Discernment will be important as you approach this work.

Finally (and maybe read this one more than once), Step 9 isn't about perfection. You'll feel awkward. You may stumble a bit. This doesn't mean you're doing the step wrong. Courage won't mean the absence of fear. Do it afraid.

So now, before we move farther into Step 9, let's pause and pray:

God, would you guide me in this step? Give me the wisdom I need to move forward in truth and love. Help me rid my heart of apologies that aren't wholehearted. Give me eyes to see all the ways I have hurt others throughout my life. Provide me with clarity and humility and courage so that I can do what would be honoring to you. I pray for the people I will contact as I seek to make amends. Would you open their hearts to hear it? I pray you'd bless their lives. Help me accept whatever response may come. I place every relationship and every attempt at amends into your worthy hands. Amen.

VIDEO NOTES

As you watch the video, use the space below to take notes. We've included some key points to get you started.

SCAN HERE TO WATCH THE VIDEO FOR STEP 9.

Step 9 moves us from willingness to action. Reconciliation and amends are not the same thing.

This step involves making direct amends to people we have harmed, wherever possible.

There are four categories for making amends with the people in your life you have harmed:

1. Now
2. Later
3. Maybe
4. Never (Indirect)

When we go to make amends, we are in charge of making amends. We are not in charge of the other person's response.

A framework for making amends can be helpful. Such as:

1. Speak directly about the harm you have caused, without excuses or defensiveness.

2. Try to understand how your actions affected the other person. Ask if there is anything else that you should be aware of.

3. Lay out the amends you want to make for the specific person you have harmed.

4. Ask if there is anything else that would be helpful.

We see this step in Scripture, in the story of the prodigal son in Luke 15:17-19 (NIV):

> When he came to his senses, he said, . . . "I will set out and go back to my father and say to him: Father, I have sinned against heaven and against you. I am no longer worthy to be called your son; make me like one of your hired servants."

DISCUSSION QUESTIONS

Use these questions to discuss in a small group or reflect individually in your workbook.

1. When you think about making amends, what emotions rise to the top for you? Are you fearful? Smug? Hesitant?

2. Recall the first activity from Step 8 in this workbook where you made a list of people you've harmed (see page 100). Which person (or persons) on your list do you find most difficult to approach? Why might that be?

3. From your perspective, what components make a good apology? How are you planning to incorporate those in your amends-making journey?

4. Where do you sense God may be nudging you toward repair? What steps might be necessary for you to get there?

5. Can you think of a time when someone approached you to make amends? How did it feel? What parts of it would you want to replicate in an apology to someone else, and what parts might you want to leave out? Why?

KEY ACTIVITIES

The Four Amends Categories

In the last step, we made a list of all the people we've harmed. Now, as we think about taking appropriate action, we'll work to categorize those people to better assess how to approach our amends.

John suggests that a helpful way to discern when and how to make amends is to create four categories: Now, Later, Maybe, Never (*Steps*, 204). These categories exist to ensure that amends are made in ways that are wise and loving and do not cause further harm. These categories are *not* to let you off the hook.

Fill in the quadrants below with the names of people on your list from Step 8, and discern the people you will first approach as well as the people you need to think and pray about. Seek counsel from a trusted friend to continue understanding the best path forward.

NOW	LATER
MAYBE	**NEVER**

Seeing Through Their Eyes

In Step 9, the soul work happens when we begin to understand the true impact of our actions on other people. So for now, pick one person you have hurt. You can start with someone on your "Now" list from the previous activity.

Pause for a moment and imagine (however painful this might be) what the other person may have felt as a result of your actions. Then complete the prompts below to honestly acknowledge the impact of your actions.

The person I hurt: ______________________________

What I did to cause this hurt:
Be concrete here. Name actions, not patterns.

Based on what I know, what harm did my actions likely cause?
Think about what the other person experienced. Perhaps you caused embarrassment, shame, or sadness.

In what ways could they have been damaged by this situation?

Finally, what could communicate to them that I genuinely see their hurt and want to make things right between us?

Preparing to Make Amends

As we prepare to actually approach the people on our list, it's helpful to have a plan in place. We don't want to be impulsive. We want to convey genuine care through preparation and thoughtfulness. Deciding what you will say ahead of time will help you demonstrate that this interaction matters to you.

Right now, we'll work on the format of one conversation based on the four-step process in *Steps* (see pages 206–207).

Fill in the prompts below to help guide what you will say during this conversation. (Of course, understand that there are nuances to each situation and this template may not be one-size-fits-all. This is just a starting point.)

> Hey, ____________________ (name), I want to talk with you about something. I realize that I ____________________________________ ____________________________ (what I did/said/failed to do), and I can see that this caused ____________________________________ ______________________________________ (impact on them). I take full responsibility for my part without excuses.
>
> I've tried to think about this from your point of view, but I would really appreciate hearing how this affected you. Is there anything you want me to understand?
>
> Here is what I'm doing to make this right: ____________________ ____. Is there anything else that would be helpful?
>
> Thank you for listening. I'm not expecting anything from you. I just want to be honest about the harm I caused and do what I can to repair it.

Practice reading this out loud a few times and see how it feels. Notice whether any part of what you wrote is about relieving your own discomfort rather than repairing harm, and revise accordingly. Pray that God would give you the ability to deliver it authentically.

Amends Readiness Check

Before moving forward, it's important to pause and examine why we're making amends. As we've discussed, Step 9 is not about relieving discomfort or securing a particular response. It's about repairing harm. It's about seeking the good of the other person and becoming someone who lives in truth and love.

This short readiness check can help ensure your heart is aligned with the purpose of this step.

Read through the statements below slowly. You don't need to answer them perfectly. Honesty is what matters here.

Ask yourself:

- Am I willing to name my specific actions without defending, explaining, or minimizing them? Y / N
- Am I prepared to listen to the other person's experience without correcting their memory or justifying myself? Y / N
- Am I making amends for their good, not to relieve my guilt or anxiety? Y / N
- Am I willing to make amends even if the relationship is not restored? Y / N
- Am I willing to make amends even if I receive no forgiveness, reassurance, or response? Y / N
- Am I open to hearing that my impact was different from my intention? Y / N
- Am I willing to accept limits if making direct amends would cause harm? Y / N

Now pause and reflect: What, if anything, about making amends feels especially hard or risky for me?

What outcome am I most attached to right now?

What might it look like to release that outcome to God?

Finally, pray this simple prayer: *God, help me seek repair rather than relief. Help me tell the truth with love. Help me do my part and trust you with the rest. Amen.*

Discerning Amends

Once we've clarified our readiness, we can begin discerning timing and approach. An important part of making amends is remembering that timing is part of love. Not every attempt to make amends should be immediate. The question is not "Do I feel ready?" but rather "Is this moment wise?"

Note: Delaying making amends is not the same as avoiding it. Wisdom asks when and how, not whether.

Reflect using these prompts:

What makes this situation delicate or complex?

What preparation do I need before I initiate contact?

Who could help me discern the right timing?

Release the Outcome

Our final activity is one of the most crucial components of this step. There's a painful truth involved in making amends that we touched on a little already: As much as you might want to, you can't control the other person's response. The only thing you can control is your own willingness to repair.

Releasing the outcome does not mean releasing responsibility. It means surrendering control over the other person's response. So right now, let's approach this with the right lens and release control.

Think of one person on your list. Then complete these sentences:

God, I surrender my need for them to respond in this way:

____.

As I make amends, help me focus on becoming a person who

____.

Now, take a moment to pray: *God, I surrender the outcome to you. Amen.*

After releasing the outcome, return your attention to the concrete action you are responsible for taking.

SCRIPTURE FOR REFLECTION

Use this section to reflect on some verses that shed light on this step. You might ask God to reveal what he wants you to take away from them.

> Make allowance for each other's faults, and forgive anyone who offends you. Remember, the Lord forgave you, so you must forgive others.
> COLOSSIANS 3:13

Think about the divine forgiveness you've been offered. How does this change the way you think about making amends with people you might have hurt?

> People who conceal their sins will not prosper,
> but if they confess and turn from them, they will receive mercy.
> PROVERBS 28:13

True confession and repentance lead to mercy. What would it feel like for you to approach making amends knowing mercy waits on the other side?

> No, O people, the LORD has told you what is good,
> and this is what he requires of you:
> to do what is right, to love mercy,
> and to walk humbly with your God.
> MICAH 6:8

Think about the three parts of this verse: doing what's right, loving mercy, and walking humbly with God. Which one seems most challenging for you? Why might that be?

CLOSING THOUGHTS

As we discussed, Step 9 takes courage. It is one of the most difficult parts of the entire journey. To make amends with the people you've hurt requires relentless honesty and humility.

Up to this point, you've identified the people you've harmed. You've looked at your actions with honesty instead of excuses. You've asked God to grow a willingness in places where fear and shame and pride once lived. And you've begun preparing for the realities that seeking repair might require.

This is hard work, to say the least.

John challenges us to "dare to be guilty" (*Steps*, 221). Through this step, we can dare to believe that love and guilt can coexist in the same heart at the same time. Moving forward, when we've done something wrong, instead of excusing it away, we can choose to acknowledge the mistake. We can name it and own it. We can believe that God will redeem even what we wish we could undo.

So . . . will you dare to be guilty?

Good. Time for Step 10.

JOURNAL SPACE

After completing this chapter, take five to ten minutes of silence. Then think through these questions in the journaling space that follows:

- What do I hope changes in me as a person through seeking to make amends?
- What might God be doing in my life right now?
- What specific next step will I take this week?

STEP 10

The Repetition: Continual Inventory

We continued to take personal inventory and when we were wrong promptly admitted it.

STEPS, PAGES 223–233

OPENING REFLECTION

The first nine steps have helped us look honestly at our past. What are our patterns? How have we shown up in life and relationships?

We've admitted our own powerlessness. We've come to believe in God and surrendered our life to him. We've taken inventory (ouch), confessed (more ouch), and become ready to ask God for help. We've prayed that he'd remove our shortcomings and started down the long road of making amends.

Here we are at Step 10, and this is about what happens next, during normal, everyday life.

God has been at work forming our character in us, and it continues now. Because now, Step 10 invites us to do more than wait for a crisis to strike or another rock-bottom moment; it invites us into a way of life in the ordinary. We don't take moral inventory of the past and just stop there, calling it good. We continue to pay attention. When we get off course, we learn to take our mistakes to God as promptly as possible and make them right.

John says it this way: "The real purpose of this step is to re-form the habits of our mind so that our thoughts remain continually directed toward God's help and guidance" (*Steps*, 227).

What we really want is to catch ourselves and our missteps as early as we can. As soon as they happen, we make them right. When we can increase our promptness in admitting defects, we can change our life and avoid slipping back into old, painful patterns. And that's good news, because that's exactly what Step 10 will teach us.

So right now, before we move farther into Step 10, let's pause and pray:

God, thank you for not leaving me to figure this out on my own. Thank you for helping me to see myself clearly. Please show me where I have been wrong in thought, word, or action. Give me courage to admit it quickly and to make things right wherever I possibly can. Teach me how to walk with you, one day, one hour at a time. Amen.

VIDEO NOTES

As you watch the video, use the space below to take notes. We've included some key points to get you started.

SCAN HERE TO WATCH THE VIDEO FOR STEP 10.

In Step 10, we continue to take personal inventory. When we are wrong, we promptly admit it, and this moves us into daily practice.

This step takes Steps 4 through 9 and helps us put them into practice on a daily basis.

The wording matters: Step 10 does not say, "*If* we were wrong." It says, "*When* we were wrong."

A way to look at spiritual growth is as decreasing the lag time between when we've done something wrong and when we've admitted it.

God will care for people one day at a time.

We do Step 10 one day at a time, with two resources to help us:

1. Daily review

2. Spot checks

When we feel confused, upset, agitated, or depressed, that can be a signal that it's time for a spot check.

The issue is never just what's going on in our circumstances. The issue is always *How am I responding to this?*

Step 10 is practiced every day for the rest of your life.

DISCUSSION QUESTIONS

Use these questions to discuss in a small group or reflect individually in your workbook.

1. When was the last time you noticed a moment when you were wrong about something? How did you respond? Was your immediate, knee-jerk reaction to defend it? If so, why do you think this is? (See John's peanut butter example in *Steps*, 227.)

2. Think about the ways you might be tempted to drift from conscious awareness of God's presence. Is it through words, actions, thoughts, relationships, or something else? Discuss or consider why that might be.

3. "I was wrong." Three small but mighty words. How could this sentence transform the relationships in your life?

4. When you think about the steps being a lifelong process, how does it make you feel? Can you relate when John talks about overwhelm that can come when we look too far into the future? (See *Steps*, 225–227.)

5. What's one way that you can live *with God* today?

KEY ACTIVITIES

The Daily Review

As you learned in *Steps*, Step 10 is the "one day at a time" step. Just as a coach will tell the players, "Win the inning, win the game," this step focuses on *this* day, this moment. It's about keeping in alignment with the Holy Spirit as we go about our life and admitting when we're wrong as quickly and as often as possible.

There are a couple of ways to approach this: daily reviews and spot checks.

Right now, we're going to practice the daily review. We're borrowing this framework from Saint Ignatius, and it involves five simple, brief parts (see *Steps*, 228–231).

Use the guided reflection below to consider your full day and practice inventorying. If you're using this workbook and it's currently morning, you can use yesterday as a review. If it's evening, review today.

1. ASK FOR GOD'S HELP

Be still for a moment. Remember that wherever you are, God is with you. Pray: *God, my help comes from you. Help me see my day as you see it.*

2. REMEMBER YOUR BLESSINGS

We don't just inventory liabilities; we inventory assets too (see *Steps*, 228). Think back through your last twenty-four hours. What specifically are you grateful for? Where did you receive grace from God? What surprised you? What made you smile? Write down a few examples.

3. PAY ATTENTION TO YOUR SIGNIFICANT FEELINGS

Sometimes our strong emotions are a window into the drift of our hearts. Think about where in your day your feelings took the biggest swings. Where did you feel joy? Sadness? Rage? Desire? Write down a few moments that come to mind.

Now, think about the feelings you experienced and recorded above. Consider this question: *Did this feeling lead me closer to God?* Respond below.

4. REJOICE IN WHAT WAS GOOD AND SEEK FORGIVENESS WHERE NEEDED

"Perfectionism . . . is a killer for the spiritual life" (*Steps*, 229). When we look equally at what went well and what we still need to work on, God's grace can turn our failings into something useful.

So right now, respond to the following prompts.

Where was I aligned with God today?

Where was I wrong and in need of forgiveness?

5. LOOK TOWARD TOMORROW

Finally, ask God to help you live your next twenty-four hours with greater awareness and love in your heart. Determine if there's a person you need to speak with, a situation you need to repair, or a pattern you want to disrupt before it carries forward.

Tomorrow, with God's help, I will . . .

This exercise may have taken a while this time, but with practice, it becomes a learned framework to check-in with yourself. Daily honesty keeps our character defects from regaining strength in our life.

I Was Wrong

A core function of Step 10 (and the lifelong Twelve Steps journey) is admitting when you were wrong. So now, let's walk through what that could look like in practice.

Think of one specific, recent situation from the last few days where you may need to own something you did. It might be something small that you'd ordinarily brush off, or it might be something really harmful. Step 10 invites us to pay attention, no matter the circumstances.

Fill in the blanks of this guided script on the next page to help you practice how to take ownership for wrongdoing. Be as specific as you can.

> Hey, ______________________ (name), I want to talk to you about something I did. I realize that when I ____________________________ ____________________________________ (what I did, said, or failed to do), I caused ____________________________________ (how it impacted the other person). I take full responsibility for my part without excuse. I am truly sorry. If there is something I can do to make this right, I am willing to hear it.

Now try reading this out loud. If this feels hard to say, you aren't alone. Even writing it down first can help soften your heart and build readiness to approach the person you harmed.

Returning to the First Three Steps

As John often reminds us, the Twelve Steps are a way of life. It's worth revisiting all of them as you continue onward, as well as this summary statement of the first three steps: "I can't. He can. I think I'll let him." This reminder is particularly helpful in Step 10 as you work to take continual inventory and make amends, one day at a time.

Right now, take a moment to consider the statement "I can't. He can. I think I'll let him." Journal about what surfaces in your heart.

Spot Check

As we discussed in the first activity, Step 10 is about doing life with God, one day at a time. There are two ways John suggests going about this (see *Steps*, 227–233). We practiced the daily review, and now we'll work on spot checks.

In this step, "we learn to pause and check ourselves quickly throughout the day as needed" (*Steps*, 231). This is about noticing in real time where we are missing the mark, not waiting until the day's end when we're reflecting at large on the entire twenty-four hours.

Often upset emotions are our warning sign. "When we get anxious, or resentful, or confused, or troubled in our conscience, it can become an invitation to take inventory and find out what is needed to 'walk with the Spirit'" (*Steps*, 231). Our ego may take the wheel through things like sharp words, jealousy, defensiveness, and so on.

Spot checks provide us the opportunity for course correction in real time. So right now, we'll consider a recent moment (preferably from today) and answer a few prompts. Ideally, we'll do this in real time when we notice a character flaw, but for now, let's practice retrospectively.

A moment I need to spot check:

The emotion or reaction I experienced:

The shortcoming beneath the surface of my action:

What I need God's help with to overcome this action or behavior:

What I'll do to restart from here or make it right:

Practice this spot check as often as needed throughout the day. Sixty seconds of honesty can provide a comeback for an entire day.

SCRIPTURE FOR REFLECTION

Use this section to reflect on some verses that shed light on this step. You might ask God to reveal what he wants you to take away from them.

> Don't worry about tomorrow, for tomorrow will bring its own worries. Today's trouble is enough for today.
>
> **MATTHEW 6:34**

What could it look like for you to truly only worry about today? What does surrendering tomorrow mean?

I look up to the mountains—
 does my help come from there?
My help comes from the LORD,
 who made heaven and earth!

He will not let you stumble;
 the one who watches over you will not slumber.
Indeed, he who watches over Israel
 never slumbers or sleeps.

The LORD himself watches over you!
 The LORD stands beside you as your protective shade.
The sun will not harm you by day,
 nor the moon at night.

The LORD keeps you from all harm
 and watches over your life.
The LORD keeps watch over you as you come and go,
 both now and forever.

PSALM 121

Remember where your help comes from. How can you keep this truth in mind this week?

> Since we are surrounded by such a huge crowd of witnesses to the life of faith, let us strip off every weight that slows us down, especially the sin that so easily trips us up. And let us run with endurance the race God has set before us.
>
> **HEBREWS 12:1**

John discusses how the apostle Paul's imperfections didn't discourage him; they motivated him (see *Steps*, 232–233). What might you learn from Paul's example?

CLOSING THOUGHTS

Spiritual transformation isn't an event; it's a way of life. Step 10 is an invitation to return to honesty over and over as often as is necessary because it's a pathway to greater freedom.

By this point, you've started to notice how old patterns and tendencies can resurface in your life. Maybe it's your tongue—you use sharp language with those you love. Maybe it's resentment—you hold people to perfectionistic standards and withhold forgiveness. Maybe it's temptation—you keep returning to specific behaviors that you know aren't serving you or bringing you closer to God.

Step 10 doesn't shame us for this. Instead, it gives us the tools to notice early, admit properly, and surrender fully to God.

John writes,

> We refuse to allow our lack of progress yesterday to negatively impact our today. We press on, like a champion running a race: looking forward, every muscle moving toward the goal to grasp the prize for which we have been grasped. We just don't quit. We keep going. Not because there are no flaws in our attempt, but because there is no other goal worth the pursuit. And because we do not run alone. (*Steps*, 233)

So we keep going. We keep returning to the truth and practicing humility. We know that we don't run alone.

And that's a good thing, because Step 11 will draw us even closer into conscious connection with God.

For today, though, simply notice and respond. Keep coming back—it works if you work it.

JOURNAL SPACE

After completing this chapter, take five to ten minutes of silence. Then think through these questions in the journaling space that follows:

- What does it mean to me that the steps are a way of life rather than a program to complete?
- What would it look like to integrate daily reviews and spot checks into my regular routines?
- What next step will I take today?

STEP 11

The Connection: The With-God Life

We sought through prayer and meditation to improve our conscious contact with God as we understood Him, praying only for knowledge of His will for us and the power to carry that out.

STEPS, PAGES 235–257

OPENING REFLECTION

Can you believe it? We're almost through this journey. Step 11 brings us to one of the most beautiful invitations of this whole process: to improve our contact with God. To live our life *with* him. To be aware of his presence in ordinary moments. To remember that we're not alone. To be open to his guidance as we move throughout our day.

Step 10 taught us to walk honestly with God day by day, and Step 11 teaches us to walk *closely* with him. Spiritual companionship is what we're after. As John puts it, this is the step where we're moving from spiritual defense to offense (see *Steps*, 237). We fill our minds and hearts with what is life-giving rather than just removing defects. And the good news is this: We're after improvement, not perfection. Simply practicing means we're getting a little better than we were.

John says it this way: "The only real antidote to fear is conscious awareness of the presence of God. Not only that, when we're living in conscious awareness of God's presence, it makes a difference in our choices" (*Steps*, 239).

We can do this through prayer and meditation, but remember, these aren't achievements. It can be tempting to try to master them or "succeed," but they're simply practices, ways of returning again and again to truth. God is here, God is good, and God is able. The goal is to open our hearts and minds to him and remember that he is always near. That's the "with-God" life Jesus lived. And it's available to us through Step 11.

So before we move farther, let's pause and pray:

God, would you draw me into a greater awareness of you and your Spirit? Would you teach me how to listen, to notice, to be still? Show me how to live this day with you and spend every moment together. Give me the willingness to do the next right thing with you. Amen.

VIDEO NOTES

As you watch the video, use the space below to take notes. We've included some key points to get you started.

SCAN HERE TO WATCH THE VIDEO FOR STEP 11.

Step 11 says, "We sought through prayer and meditation to improve our conscious contact with God as we understood Him, praying only for knowledge of His will for us and the power to carry that out."

It doesn't say *perfect* our conscious contact with God. It just says *improve*.

If right now you only have conscious contact with God one time a day and tomorrow you do it two times a day, you have doubled your conscious contact with God. You're doing great.

The first ten steps are playing defense. In Step 11, we go on offense.

Dallas Willard writes, "The greatest human freedom, the one freedom that no one can take away from you, however much they might be able to control your body, is the freedom of where we will place our minds."

We have the ability to place our minds where they can be nurtured with strength and love and joy so that peace flows out of us.

Nothing defeats prayer faster than obligation and guilt.

Two tools for Step 11 are prayer and meditation.

A key question for prayer is *Am I praying in such a way that it makes me want to pray?* If not, then we need to find another way.

Prayer is talking with God about what we're doing together.

It is quite easy for us to think that prayer is about trying to get God to do what we want, and then when that doesn't happen, we conclude that prayer "doesn't work."

Meditation is simply sustained thought.

If you can worry, you already know how to meditate. Worry is described as toxic meditation.

That's Step 11: talking with God about what we're doing together and meditating by placing our minds where we want them to be to improve our conscious contact with God.

DISCUSSION QUESTIONS

Use these questions to discuss in a small group or reflect individually in your workbook.

1. What does being in conscious contact with God mean to you? When are you most frequently in contact with God?

2. Is it easier for you to talk to God or listen to him? Why might that be?

3. Step 11 is not about getting God's attention but about giving him ours. How might that change the way you pray?

4. What are some new ways you could notice God in the ordinary moments of your day-to-day life?

5. What might change in your life if you asked, "God, what would please you most right now?" several times a day?

KEY ACTIVITIES

Train Your Thoughts

In chapter 11A, John talks about the importance of examining our thought life. Often, what we're thinking is what influences our actions and behavior patterns.

John writes,

> We cannot change what we cannot see, including our own thoughts. So if we're going to improve our conscious contact with God, we want to become more aware of what it is we're normally thinking about, what our minds *are* in conscious contact with. Managing our consciousness—our thoughts and our inner awareness—is the ultimate challenge of life. (*Steps*, 240)

Spend a few minutes gently noticing where your mind has naturally gone over the last day.

As you write, resist the urge to judge or evaluate what you notice. Instead, imagine God sitting with you, interested but unalarmed. Relaxed. Loving. Grace-filled.

Ask yourself: What does my mind return to when I'm not trying to control it?

Fleeing from Denial

In chapter 11B, John tells a story about two maggots (see *Steps*, 245). One maggot takes the credit for something that isn't his to claim. Reference the story and then consider: Is there an area of your life where you may have been wrongly taking the credit? This matters, because we're not meant to live on the power of our own strength. Remember Steps 1 through 3? I can't. He can. I think I'll let him.

Journal now about what comes to mind. How might acknowledging God's role here invite gratitude rather than shame?

Guided Meditation

Meditation is a practice we can use to come into conscious contact with God. John writes that meditation "is simply sustained thought" (*Steps*, 249). Right now, we'll practice meditation using the framework from chapter 11B. A quick note, though: If at any point this feels heavy, forced, or discouraging, you may stop. As we learned, prayer that makes us want to avoid God is not the goal.

First, get still. Be quiet. Dim the distractions and relax your body.

Then ask God to bring you peace. Take some deep breaths and pay attention to any anxiety or fear that surfaces. Set it aside for now.

Next, John suggests taking Scripture and reflecting on its meaning (see *Steps*, 250). Think about its context, its application, its layers. Ask where you reflect it in your life and where you resist it. Talk to God all the while about where your mind goes.

Finally, ask God if there is anything he wants you to know. Sit quietly and listen for an answer. Then thank him for his love.

If nothing came to mind, or your thoughts wandered the entire time, that is not failure. The practice is returning again tomorrow.

If thoughts or feelings surfaced, use the space below to write them down.

Do the Next Right Thing

In chapter 11C, John encourages us to pay attention to God's will for our life through conscious contact and then to carry it out. On page 257, he gives some examples of what that might look like:

- Write someone a note.
- Give someone a gift.
- Relax.
- Drive slower.
- Volunteer.
- Ask for help.

Pick something that makes sense for you. Is there a small, ordinary action that feels consistent with love, peace, or attentiveness today? This is not about certainty. It's about responsiveness. Whether it's an action from this list or something the Spirit gives you right now, take a moment to write it down and make a plan for how to act on it.

SCRIPTURE FOR REFLECTION

Use this section to reflect on some verses that shed light on this step. You might ask God to reveal what he wants you to take away from them.

> Be still, and know that I am God!
> I will be honored by every nation.
> I will be honored throughout the world.
>
> **PSALM 46:10**

How proficient are you at practicing stillness?

> Remain in me [Jesus], and I will remain in you. For a branch cannot produce fruit if it is severed from the vine, and you cannot be fruitful unless you remain in me.
>
> Yes, I am the vine; you are the branches. Those who remain in me, and I in them, will produce much fruit. For apart from me you can do nothing.
>
> **JOHN 15:4-5**

How does this verse shape your understanding of conscious contact with God?

> Never stop praying.
> **1 THESSALONIANS 5:17**

Think about the concept of ceaseless prayer. What could that look like in your life?

CLOSING THOUGHTS

Step 11 teaches us how to live our life *with* God in everyday life. Daily. Hourly. Minute by minute.

The invitation in this step is simple: *Improve* your conscious contact with God. Not perfect it, just improve it. You don't have to be "good" at prayer to pray. You don't have to be a master at meditation to be able to sit in silence. You don't even always have to *feel* God's presence to be *in* God's presence. He's always there. The work of this step is learning to notice.

As we learned, the greatest freedom we have is the freedom to choose what we allow our minds to dwell on. When we deliberately decide to turn our minds toward what is true, what is good, and what is life-giving, we discover that God has been present all along.

Step 11 is about spiritual companionship. It's about learning to pray honestly, listen humbly, meditate patiently, and seek God wholeheartedly. We seek God in obedience and carry out his will through the way we actually live.

So turn toward God, because he's turning toward you. Seek conscious contact with the one who knows you. He loves you, and he wants to do life with you. And as this awareness begins to take shape in your life, you may notice that you start wanting to share it with others.

That's where Step 12 comes in.

JOURNAL SPACE

After completing this chapter, take five to ten minutes of silence. Then think through these questions in the journaling space that follows:

- In what ways do I already attempt to make conscious contact with God?
- What is one step I can take to improve my conscious contact with God today?
- What could it look like to practice prayer and meditation in the normal flow of my everyday life?

STEP 12

The Vocation: Helping Others

Having had a spiritual awakening, we tried to carry this message to others, and to practice these principles in all our affairs.

STEPS, PAGES 259–277

OPENING REFLECTION

Step 12 . . . You made it!

Take a deep breath. Look back for a moment at how far you've come.

You've walked through confession and clarity, trust and vulnerability. You've inventoried and made amends and surrendered and surrendered again.

Your faithfulness is changing you, one day, one decision at a time.

That you are here at the final step is a testament to God's love and your willingness to follow him. Thus comes the invitation of the final step: Now we carry this message to others.

John writes, "Sometimes we will hear the saying, 'You cannot give what you do not have.' And that is true. But in spiritual life, so is the reverse: 'You cannot keep what you do not give'" (*Steps*, 263).

The purpose of a spiritual awakening isn't just personal transformation. The Twelve Steps exist so that we can be personally transformed, yes, but so that we can help others heal too. Our life is not our own; we're meant to lay it down. The steps exist because when we turn our focus outward and help other people become better, we become more like Jesus. We simply offer who we are becoming in service to the people around us.

Step 12 is a way of life more than it is a finish line—there's no such thing on this journey. It's a daily posture. It's a continual walk with God, living in surrender, practicing all that we've learned. And now you're equipped to do the long work of consistently walking with and noticing God.

So let's look at the final step and remember that this journey is really a gift we are meant to give away.

Before moving forward, pause and pray:

God, thank you for bringing me this far. I can't do this without you. Thank you for the awakening you began in me. May it continue so that I can help awaken others by your Spirit. Help me love with the same grace you have shown me. Amen.

VIDEO NOTES

As you watch the video, use the space below to take notes. We've included some key points to get you started.

SCAN HERE TO WATCH THE VIDEO FOR STEP 12.

Step 12 says, "Having had a spiritual awakening, we tried to carry this message to others, and to practice these principles in all our affairs."

A "spiritual awakening" is when we become aware of the spiritual reality of the presence of God.

This happens amid our ordinary experiences of gratitude, awe, guilt, wanting to make something right, purpose, calling, love. We have spiritual awakenings all the time, but we just don't know what to name them.

We see this in Genesis with Jacob at Bethel. "Surely the LORD is in this place, and I was not aware of it" (Genesis 28:16, NIV).

Remember, the steps are not a self-improvement program. They're not something we are doing to get an outcome we want. They are a process by which we are receiving power to be restored to sobriety and to have a life of freedom and power.

Why carry this message to others? Not because there are other needy, weak people out there. This comes from Mark 10:43-45: "Whoever wants to become great among you must become your servant, and whoever wants to be first must be slave of all. For even the Son of Man did not come to be served, but to serve" (NIV).

Bill W. learned that the only way to keep it is to give it away.

If you keep it, you lose it; that is the teaching of Jesus.

DISCUSSION QUESTIONS

Use these questions to discuss in a small group or reflect individually in your workbook.

1. What does "You have to give it away to keep it" (*Steps*, 263) mean to you? Do you struggle to give yourself or your possessions away? Explain.

2. As the AA refrain goes, "It works if you work it." John points out that the latter half of that statement—"if you work it"—is where it gets hard. Think of a scenario in your life where you've struggled to maintain a commitment you made. What happened? How will you overcome that on this journey?

3. When you think about paying forward all that you've learned, what parts energize you? What hesitations or concerns do you have?

4. Where do you sense God nudging you to serve, listen, encourage, or walk alongside someone else?

KEY ACTIVITIES

Your Awakening Story

On page 267 of *Steps*, John invites us to consider the trials we've experienced in life. Often the hurts, the struggles, and the pain are actually what most unite us with others.

Take a few minutes now and write down some of the biggest trials you've overcome already. You never know. These painful experiences may just be the lifeline someone in your future needs to hear. Also note that this is not a performance—you may never even share these words with anyone. This exercise is about noticing what God has done in your life and being open to how he may use it in the future.

Now, fill in the blanks to start crafting your story:

Before I did the Twelve Steps, my life felt . . .

Through these steps, God has shown me . . .

One change in me that I am grateful for is . . .

One way my experience might be useful to someone else is . . .

It Works If You Work It

What part of the statement "It works if you work it" most challenges you? Reflect for a few minutes and journal below about what you discover.

The Promises

So much of the Twelve Steps journey is about celebrating personal inadequacy. However, that is not the destination. Inadequacy doesn't get the last word (see *Steps*, 275). The Twelve Steps offer us Twelve Promises. (You can reference these in chapter 12C of *Steps*.)

Promise #1: We are going to know a new freedom and a new happiness.
Promise #2: We will not regret the past nor wish to shut the door on it.
Promise #3: We will comprehend the word *serenity*.
Promise #4: We will know peace.

Promise #5: No matter how far down the scale we have gone, we will see how our experience can benefit others.
Promise #6: The feeling of uselessness and self-pity will disappear.
Promise #7: We will lose interest in selfish things and gain interest in our fellows.
Promise #8: Self-seeking will slip away.
Promise #9: Our whole attitude and outlook upon life will change.
Promise #10: Fear of people and economic insecurity will leave us.
Promise #11: We will intuitively know how to handle situations that used to baffle us.
Promise #12: We will suddenly realize that God is doing for us what we could not do for ourselves.

These promises describe the slow, fulfilling by-product of a life lived in surrender. Which one of them most moves you? Why do you think that is? Circle or underline it above and then reflect on it below.

The Five-Second Practice

In chapter 12C, John issues a challenge, and it only takes five seconds to implement it into your day. Check out his thoughts on how to infuse hope each morning:

> The promises remind us that we were made for hope and cannot live without it. It is particularly important for us to have hope at the beginning of each day. So this is a five-second habit that you can incorporate into your life that can make a significant impact.
>
> When you wake up in the morning and your feet hit the ground, let your first words be "This is the day that the Lord has made; I will rejoice and be glad in it."

> Here's why it works. It is attached to something you're already doing (you have to get up anyway). It is super easy to do. It lifts up the heart. (*Steps*, 276)

Some mornings this will feel true, and other mornings you might struggle with it. But like so much of this journey, it's about willingness and surrender. So right now, no matter what time of day it is, take a moment to write those words down: "This is the day that the Lord has made. I will rejoice and be glad in it" (see Psalm 118:24). When you wake up tomorrow, practice saying it first thing, and experience the hope that comes when you take the words to heart.

SCRIPTURE FOR REFLECTION

Use this section to reflect on some verses that shed light on this step. You might ask God to reveal what he wants you to take away from them.

> Give as freely as you have received!
> **MATTHEW 10:8**

Where in your life have you personally received freely? Where now can you give freely in return?

> Is there any encouragement from belonging to Christ? Any comfort from his love? Any fellowship together in the Spirit? Are your hearts tender and compassionate? Then make me truly happy by agreeing wholeheartedly with each other, loving one another, and working together with one mind and purpose.
>
> Don't be selfish; don't try to impress others. Be humble, thinking of others as better than yourselves. Don't look out only for your own interests, but take an interest in others, too.
>
> You must have the same attitude that Christ Jesus had.
>
> **PHILIPPIANS 2:1-5**

Humility is required to serve others. How does this verse shape your desire to do so?

> All praise to God, the Father of our Lord Jesus Christ. God is our merciful Father and the source of all comfort. He comforts us in all our troubles so that we can comfort others. When they are troubled, we will be able to give them the same comfort God has given us.
>
> **2 CORINTHIANS 1:3-4**

Reflect on some of the ways God has comforted you. How does that comfort equip you to help others?

CLOSING THOUGHTS

You may have reached Step 12, but this is not the end. This is the beginning of a new way of living. And as John teaches, "Whether you're in a peak or a trough . . . remember: it's temporary" (*Steps*, 273).

Take a moment right now to consider all you've done. Think through the progress you've made on this journey: You've faced truths you once avoided. You've come eye-to-eye with character deficiencies and chosen to relish reality. You've surrendered the parts of you that you tightly clung to. You've walked into really, really difficult things: forgiveness, confession, making amends, and daily transformation.

The Twelve Steps take courage. They require humility and grace and brutal honesty. And you've risen to the challenge. You are not now who you were when you began. That's a big deal.

We're all invited to a different way of life with Jesus, one that is externally focused, where personal healing becomes someone else's hope. When we carry the message of hope forward, sometimes even simply by who we're becoming, others are forever changed.

So keep walking. Keep practicing. Keep surrendering.

Keep coming back.

It works if you work it.

JOURNAL SPACE

After completing this chapter, take five to ten minutes of silence. Then think through these questions in the journaling space that follows:

- What has God changed in me through this Twelve Steps journey?
- What final thoughts come to mind about the Twelve Steps?
- What next step will I take today?

STEP 13

The Unofficial Final Step

STEPS, PAGES 279–280

We may have covered the Twelve Steps, but there is an unofficial thirteenth step to consider. That is the spiritual reality beyond Step 12. The journey does not end when we complete the list. Your growth doesn't stop when this workbook runs out of activities or pages. Personal transformation is a lifelong process.

John writes, "In the early days of the recovery movement, old-timers would sometimes refer to an unwritten thirteenth step. It came when someone who had been bravely seeking to follow the Twelve Steps reached the end of their life and died sober. They were said to have 'taken the thirteenth step'—the final step, into the grave" (*Steps*, 279).

This is the thirteenth step. It's carrying out the faithful, lifelong journey of transformation. It's the ongoing practice of the principles you've learned here. Step 13 is long surrender, focused humility, diligent dependence on God. It's trusting that the work he began in you will be carried through to completion.

The one who brought you this far will never leave you.

FINAL ENCOURAGEMENTS

1. YOU ARE NOT DONE. AND THAT IS GOOD NEWS.

Spiritual formation never has a finish line. There will be days of drift, days of despair, and days of delight. But yesterday doesn't determine today or tomorrow. The Twelve Steps are not about never failing again but about never failing to get back up.

2. YOU ARE NOT ALONE.

You didn't complete the steps alone, and you won't be alone as you continue walking through life with God. You are now one of millions of people who have walked this path and were better for it.

3. WHAT GOD STARTED, HE INTENDS TO CONTINUE.

Even if you feel like you're at risk of slipping into an old pattern, remember that you now have the tools you need to get back on track. What God started in your life he wants to bring to completion. You are not who you were, and your spirit is being formed, one day at a time.

4. IF YOU'RE WONDERING, *NOW WHAT?* THAT'S NORMAL.

Stay honest. Stay dependent on the Father. Stay connected with community. Stay attuned to the Spirit in your life. And stay hopeful. There is so much hope. Keep going.

A FINAL ACTIVITY

Complete this workbook with a simple reflection.

Take a deep breath. Then look back, look within, look ahead, and look up.

Look Back

Think about who you were at the beginning of this journey. What was different in you then?

Look Within

What parts of your character have been most changed through the Twelve Steps?

Look Ahead

Where do you hope the continued pursuit of the Twelve Steps will take you and your life?

Look Up

Thank God for his love and kindness toward you.

About the Authors

John Ortberg is a bestselling author and speaker who has been in ministry for over forty years, teaching around a central theme of spiritual formation. His deep desire is for people to know God in an interactive, life-transforming way. John's books include *Steps*, *Eternity Is Now in Session*, *Soul Keeping*, *The Life You've Always Wanted*, *Faith and Doubt*, and *If You Want to Walk on Water, You've Got to Get Out of the Boat*. Presently, John leads the ministry Become New, focused on helping people grow spiritually one day at a time. Born and raised in Rockford, Illinois, John graduated from Wheaton College. He holds a master of divinity and a doctorate in clinical psychology from Fuller Seminary, and he did postgraduate work at the University of Aberdeen, Scotland. He and his wife, Nancy, live in California.

Alyssa Chandler is a writer and editor with Become New, where she has worked closely with John Ortberg for five years, developing spiritual formation resources. Her work is informed by nearly a decade of ministry experience and centers on how small, faithful practices produce real change over time. She lives in Fort Myers, Florida, with her husband and two young daughters and is continually learning what formation looks like in the midst of everyday family life.